W9-CXT-845

INVENTORY

The Book of

Stillmeadow

Also available in Large Print by
Gladys Taber:

Still Cove Journal

The Book of
Stillmeadow

Gladys Taber

G.K.HALL &CO.
Boston, Massachusetts
1984

Copyright 1937, 1938, 1939, 1940, 1941, 1942, 1943,
1944, 1945, 1946, 1947 by the Curtis Publishing
Company.

Copyright 1948 by Gladys Taber.

Published in Large Print by arrangement with
Harper & Row, Publishers

Set in 18 pt Times Roman

Library of Congress Cataloging in Publication Data

Taber, Gladys Bagg, 1899–
  The book of Stillmeadow.

  "Published in large print"—T.p. verso.
  1. Taber, Gladys, Bagg, 1899–   —Homes and
haunts—Connecticut.
  2. Authors, American—20th century—Biography.
  3. Country life—Connecticut.   4. Large type
books.   I. Title.
[PS3539.A136Z463 1984] 818'.5209 [B] 84–8936
ISBN 0–8161–3717–X (lg. print)

This Book is Written for

A little white house in the hills of New England,
The various folk who have called it home,
The friends who have graced it with love and laughter,
The cocker spaniels bouncing in the doorway,
And two cats asleep on the hearth.

THE WAY WE bought our house in the country would have turned the blood of any expert in home-buying to glacial ice. We had read some dozen books of advice and hundreds of pamphlets, it is true, and we did know that a place advertised as having deep maple shade had no plumbing. Old colonial with five fireplaces, Dutch oven, old hardware, usually meant the roof was falling in and dry rot eating the bones of the timbers. Trout stream indicated half of the yard was a swamp.

Jill had warned me against being too impulsive, a house once bought was solid and tangible as asset or as liability. It also involved mortgages. All I knew of mortgages was that in stories they were always about to be foreclosed and the hero stepped in and saved them.

Jill spoke of upkeep too, in hushed tones. And taxes.

But we went on dreaming. At the time

our family consisted of Bob, my husband, Cicely, my daughter, Jill, my sister, and Jill's two children, Don and Dorothy. And Star, Sister, and Rip, the three first family cockers. And one large tank of tropical fish. The children were little, Don being the baby of the family.

We had apartments in New York, and Bob and Jill worked while I was what we always called an idle housewife. Looking back on that period it seems to me I was always standing at the corner by Riverside Church waiting for Don to emerge in his blue bunny suit to be escorted to his home, or standing at the corner of West 108th waiting for Cicely to emerge in her red coat from P.S. 165, or standing on the corner of 110th waiting for Dorothy who needed new shoes.

Or walking Star and Sister in the park.

A week-end place in the country where we could lie out in the sun all day and the children waxed brown and vigorous, sounded like rainbow's end.

That February day we were en route to a dog show in Massachusetts with Rip, who was listed elegantly as Blue Waters Ripplemark. Rip was a beautiful blue roan parti-color, and he was carsick, and

2

recovering from a stomach upset besides. He was wrapped and muffled and throned on a hot-water bottle.

The snow had stopped before we got to Danbury.

"I saw a house advertised in the Times," said Jill. "It's near our road. We might ask about it and get some hot coffee."

A dark wind was icing the breath. The sky was the color of the inside of a coal mine. The hills of snow rose and fell, rose and fell. All the trees were held in the death of winter.

"I doubt we can get into the place," said the real estate agent, "we'll have to walk."

We walked. We walked knee-deep in snow and icy water, along a country road, leaning against the bitter wind.

"I haven't a key yet," said the agent, "we'll have to get in through the cellar."

We struggled through the last drift and almost fell into the chasm of the cellarway. And if there is anything colder than a shut house in winter, I don't know what it could be. We came up the steep broken stairs and walked into the main room with the great fireplace right beside

3

us, the hand-hewn stone smoky with years of fire, the hand-wrought crane rusty, with Dutch oven cobwebbed. The great hearthstone had sagged. A rusted iron kettle swung over dead ashes.

"This is it," I said, "we'll take it."

Six days later we made the down payment.

I really wasn't being impulsive, I told the family; I just knew it was our house.

We bought it, then, without knowing how good the beams were, what the water supply was like, how often the cellar flooded, whether the roof leaked when it showered or only when it really rained, how much of the plumbing was cracked by freezing, whether the land was worth anything, or how much the taxes would be.

We knew the house had been built around 1690, that we had forty acres, more or less. (And believe it or not, in our case it turned out to be more!) And we knew we could buy it because some people are allergic to the idea of living in a house where a murder and suicide had recently caused it to be salable.

"But they were such nice people," said the agent. "It isn't as if they were just

4

ordinary people who murdered; they were just lovely." The ghosts never bothered us. I used to listen for their voices on still summer nights. They had loved our house, that I knew. And I felt they were happy because we were giving it life again.

An old house must have the dreams and hopes and fears and sorrows of all the long-gone people in it, and to me, the sense of lives lived under my roof before me is a pleasant and comfortable thing. I never really saw our own ghosts, but I felt them.

And we pieced the story together as we sorted old letters, packed faded clothes, stacked old books. They were young, she was beautiful. He was a flyer in the first world war, he was "strange," the country people said.

He called her Laurie, which was not her name.

And one night he shot her and then shot himself and our house saw the end of a passionate and tragic story, and his love letters to her drifted across the cold floor and her orders for garden seeds that year gathered dust on her desk.

"I have a feeling Laurie does not want

us to open up that closed fireplace," I kept saying. "It's the only thing we've done I have a feeling about. She does not approve."

"Nonsense, you've been scrubbing floors too much, you're getting fanciful," said Bob.

So we tore out the brick and stone and opened it up. And when we started a small furnace fire to take the damp out of the walls, all the smoke poured happily out of the yawning hole, for the furnace flue went up that particular chimney.

"You see," I said, "I told you so."

We closed it up. But masons did not cost sixteen dollars a day that spring.

The problem of money was simple. We took all we had for the first payment on the mortgage and hoped for the best. The remodeling job which many people undergo was just not for us.

We had a mason repair the chimney so we wouldn't burn the house down before it was paid for, and we had a local carpenter take up the floorboards which were patched with Lucky Strike cigarette tins and put in new ones. We used green chestnut home-sawed and it

6

curled up at once.

We found a cleaning woman for twenty-five cents an hour and with her help Jill and I repapered the entire house and painted or washed all the woodwork and shellacked the floors. We did this in ten days.

We worked sixteen hours a day. We used paper at twenty-five cents a roll except for one extravagant piece at a dollar twenty-five for the front living room. We learned how to paper by papering.

Previous to this time, we had always "worked with our heads," as George says. George was our neighbor across the road. There were three boys, Frank, George and William. And sometimes now we wonder whether we could have managed our project at all except for them. Frank ploughed, mowed, chopped logs, fixed wiring, moved the immovable rocks until he married and moved away. Then William took over, and when he went away George stayed home to run the farm and help us keep Stillmeadow from falling apart in his off hours.

Now, when people ask me what I consider absolutely essential to country subsistence living, I say, "Somebody across the road like George and William."

When the "electric" goes off, I move to the fence and begin to yell, "George! George!" When the grass catches fire after Jill has been burning weeds, we say, "Run for George." When the sink is frozen, I say, "Better find George."

When the car won't run, we just wait for William.

When the lawn mower motor dies, we wheel the giant over to wait for William to come home.

And when we are snowed in, George digs us out.

Of course, we didn't have forethought enough to investigate the neighbors ahead of time. We just moved in and there were the boys, to be our dearest friends and greatest help down the years.

We had a well which hadn't gone dry in a hundred years. Everybody said so. So it went dry almost at once; just as soon, in fact as we got the family moved in for the summer and began the habit of bathing. We carried water from George's spring for some time. Then we found a second surface well in the front yard, and Frank hooked it up to the pump so we could alternate the wells. We couldn't afford a driven well, and this worked very well. It still does.

The first summer we learned a good deal about life in the country. It did not consist of lying in the sun, or under the old apple trees. It consisted of working until we could just stagger to bed.

A home in the country is no place for the idle. For it takes you over. Still-meadow has been a dictator for all these years. The house demands whatever it feels like and ours not to question why, ours but to do and die. The land itself does the same.

Sometimes country dwellers get help, more often they do not. Our experience has been that we worked harder when we had help than any other time. We have had a housekeeper (after the mortgage finally was paid off), a Finnish couple (for a week), a girl who brought her horse to work, one wonderful colored cook reft away by circumstances, one cook with an adolescent daughter who drove us mad and one man who mowed the lawn one day and Honey tore his pants.

And one fifteen-year-old from a church work camp who broke our hearts because her parents would not let us adopt her. One fifteen-year-old who combed her hair all day and sat in the sun looking at Don.

Now we have a philosophy. We advise our friends who want to get out of it all to plan to put all the money for servants' wages into all the equipment available and resign themselves.

A washing machine does not have to be taken ten miles to the train to go away for the week-end when you have ten guests coming. An ironer does not go to bed with a pain and have to have trays lugged up to it. A deep-freeze will give you a chef's banquet in thawing time.

We buy all the gadgets that come on the market; liquidizers, beaters, electric brooms, waffle irons, water heaters, lawn mowers, rototillers, and if we had a budget, which we haven't, the cost of all this would go in the household help column.

We have five or six radios and an electric record player, which go in with equipment and service because we don't mind fixing beans if we can listen to the best music in the world.

The first years we made do with what we had. We always refer to them as the years when Jill and I had no underwear. Our stockings and other "intimate apparel" really were in such a state that we worried constantly for fear we might be in an accident and what would the ambulance people think? We had about one good dress apiece and one hat.

But we had Stillmeadow. And we feel more than ever that the best handmade lace wears out, the night club smoke evaporates, but the hot-water heater still is as good as new. And the asparagus bed is better than ever.

The years have brought us enough leisure, at night, to read all the country books. We know all about *Ploughman's Folly, Friends of the Land,* Mr. Ed Robinson's many pamphlets. There may be one country book we do not have; if so, we just do not know of its being published.

The river of time has flowed along. The iris border has to be moved, the raspberry bed needs resetting. There was the hurricane year when we saw the gracious old apple trees fall like jackstraws. There was the tomato blight, rotting the rich crimson globes on the vine. There were the wasps, and the invasion of the black wood ants, and the time Saxon brought home the best hen from across the road.

Stillmeadow had a really good barn, and two smaller outbuildings once used for pheasants. We cleaned up the pheasant houses and made a summer house for Cicely and Dorothy and a good storage house of the larger one. Cicely and Dorothy still call theirs "the pheasant house," although we made an abortive effort to call it "the annex." Nothing ever came of this.

The barn was large enough to become a kennel for the increasing bevy of cockers. Rip and Sister and Star were happy in the house, and then we thought puppies would be wonderful. Puppies are. Sometime later we counted thirty-five cockers on our place. We bred and raised many, and always kept the ones we just couldn't part with. The idea was that the cockers would help with that last payment on the mortgage, but it didn't work out quite that way. It turned out that we worked harder to support the ones we just had to have because we loved them so much. As a commercial kennel we were an absolute flop.

Of course we couldn't sell Pussy, or Snow In Summer, or Windy Dawn, or Saxon, although once when we were at our lowest financial ebb someone offered us any sum at all for Saxon, anything. I simply retired to my bedroom and shut the door. There was not, I felt, money enough in the world to buy Saxon, no matter what.

This is not the ideal temperament for a kennel owner.

It is possible to make money on dogs, but not if you are the way we are.

We finally compromised by having one or two litters a year, and keeping only one puppy from a litter. And we remodeled the barn for a kennel, with an oil heater in winter so that whatever dogs were not in the house could stay comfortably in their own habitation. The house dogs began to take turns by the time we had not only Star and Rip and Sister, but Saxon, Pussy, Clover, Snow, Honey and Windy. And the younger ones, Melody, Hildegarde and Silver.

Then we completed the household with

Tigger, the black and rugged Connecticut Manx, and Esmé, the royal Siamese princess.

Our venture with hens did not begin until the middle of the war when the cockers needed fresh eggs to supplement a war diet. We moved in twenty-one hens and had nineteen eggs a day for some time. At its lowest, the flock produced half a dozen eggs a day. Finally, at three years of age, the hens were retired to the deep-freeze to become roasters and fricassee and arroz con pollo. Currently, we are ready for broilers.

Other livestock seemed impossible, on account of that little matter of slaughtering. The hens we could bundle up in sacks and take to Watertown to the butcher. Country-living experts always recommend rabbits, ducks, geese, pigs and maybe pigeons, too.

We know we would only make pets of them and have more mouths to feed.

Gardening is different. We began to raise vegetables the second summer, just as soon as the house was really habitable, the barn repaired and the lawn reclaimed from being a hayfield. We raised and canned enough vegetables for

14

the year for a family of six plus dozens of guests. We canned with a hot-water bath and we canned everything.

We had never raised so much as a radish before, but we learned that too. When pressure cookers dawned on the horizon, we bought the biggest size and canned with that. And when the deep-freeze was developed, we bought the biggest size available.

With an adequate deep-freeze unit, the country dweller is as near to being self-contained as anyone on this earth could be. You put down fresh-picked fruits and vegetables in the peak of their season and have them for the year round. Fresh strawberries and asparagus and peas in January, for instance. And if you don't butcher, you can buy meat in quantities and freeze it. You can freeze bread and butter and pastries and cakes and cookies, too.

And home-baked beans and squash creole and seafood casseroles. In season we send for oysters fresh from Long Island and freeze them in pints and quarts, and we make forays to Saybrook for lobsters and swordfish steaks and clams to freeze.

We freeze roasting chickens all stuffed and turkeys ready for the oven and ducklings with apple and onion filling.

We freeze leftovers too, and have extra meals from them.

And soups and tomato juice and mixed vegetables for stew. But we do not freeze potatoes or eggs or milk. Potatoes seem rubbery, we think, and eggs have to be separated and fussed around with too much. Milk we get fresh.

Unexpected company never worries us any more. Jill makes a trip to the cellar and comes up with an armful of frozen specialties. I turn the electric fan on them, and they defrost rapidly.

We try to keep broilers and a special coffee cake for Faith Baldwin and Gonnie, so when they drop in they get something they like. We put down extra barbecued lima beans for Cicely and her Latin-American friends.

There are dozens of books about country living, and many of them are really good. Of course, our favorite is *Mr. Blandings Builds His Dream House,* which ought to discourage anyone from moving away from the city, but really doesn't. It's a good book to read before sallying out to buy that dream house.

How much does it cost to live in the country? So many people ask this. This all depends on what you want. It is hardly possible to buy, repair, and move into a house in the country and make a fortune out of the land on the basis of knowing a lot about Chaucer, Shakespeare or Semantics. It is possible to have a subsistence farm if you don't mind work. This means that most of your living comes from your own land, plus a small cash income. You can raise your own food with the exception of staples such as coffee, sugar, flour, soap, and so on. You cannot raise commercial crops without a plough and a man strong enough to run that plough.

The best way to realize something from your land is to raise your own vegetables and fruits and develop one or two special crops such as asparagus or raspberries which you can market. There will always be a market for luxury edibles, packaged nicely, and fresh. County agents will help advise what your section of the country will support best. Jill is playing with the idea of Christmas trees this season; you set them out and just wait seven years and there you are!

But the main thing, in this era of chaos, is that you can be sure you won't starve. At least not until the atom bomb falls in your corn patch.

And the feeling of walking on your own land and knowing you belong to it is the only security left in today's civilization. My own recipe for world peace is a bit of land for everyone.

I began to keep a kind of diary the year we found Stillmeadow. There were so many things we wanted not to forget and the family liked a journal to refer to. Sometimes it was recipes, directions for doing over the old furniture we had bought at the auction, notes about the puppies. And sometimes it was my own thoughts, a record of country living. It turned out to be a kind of potpourri of happenings at Stillmeadow.

And after nine years, it was filling so many scrapbooks that the cupboard was full. So I made a selection of the parts that would represent our life in the country and copied it out — a staggering task.

And now we have the Book of Still-meadow.

November

Song for November

The summer leaves have spent their singing
    green,
The upland meadows lie all harvested,
Where the sweet phlox and marigold have
    been,
A late and lonely larkspur lifts her head.
This is the hour that sadly speaks of
    change,
And when the heart beats lowly in the
    night,
When morning ebbs in mist, and noon is
    strange,
And the bright birds describe their
    southward flight.

Brief days draw in a scanter measure of
    hours,
While we, with love's own season still
    unspent,
Walk alien through a world of shattered
    flowers,
And hear dark presage in the wind's
    lament.

Let us believe that love alone may be
Endowed with summer for eternity.

AUTUMN HAS VARIED gifts here in the Pomperaug Valley. Outdoor pleasures are still with us; picnics on a warm gray ledge with the good smell of broiling pork chops; walks along the country roads with the racing cockers; digging in the yet amiable earth to put in the last bulbs. We can work outdoors and not be muffled to the nose in woollens. But the lazy feeling of hot summer is gone, and we really feel like cleaning the garage, scrubbing the kennels, doing over that old maple chair.

And the indoor delights begin again too. For night draws down chill, and the open fire comes into its own. The evenings call for crisp apples and plenty of hot popcorn in bowls on the old hearth; for reading aloud, for folk songs on the phonograph.

One of the most wonderful things in the world is a full woodshed. Here in the valley we earn it. We chop and split and gather driftwood and stack logs, and it is hard and heavy work for those of us who are what our farm boys call "a little weak." But what a satisfaction to stretch out by a good substantial blaze and know the blisters on our hands were worth it!

Every type of wood has a special way of burning. Chestnut is slow and firm and has a happy faculty of "holding over" so breakfast toast can be made on the long wrought-iron fork. Maple is a good wood to burn. Apple wood smells the sweetest and is my favorite; the ghost of apple blossoms lingers in the old gnarled logs. One season we had to burn some red cedar from land clearing and the fire was hot and quick, but the cedar popped so violently that it was as if we had target practice in the house all day. It makes a nervous fire.

I am happy with the apple wood because the old trees were dead and would soon rot away, and now they go out in a glory. With the regular chestnut and maple I am always uneasily wondering whether the tree had to die, had to be cut.

Birch makes a splendor on the hearth, but we have no birch here. In Wisconsin, when I was a child, we always had dead birch trees to take care of. The white silver bursts into instant flame and is exciting, but often the heart of the log is already soggy with decay.

A house with no fireplace is a house without a heart. A fireplace should be used as a real center of family living. In summer it may be too hot to cook over the embers, but as soon as autumn blows down the hills of time, the hearth comes again to the purpose it was made for. On crisp fall mornings there will be enough embers left to make perfect toast, faintly smoky and just tender enough. Sunday morning, sausage and scrambled eggs are good, ladled from the smallest three-legged iron spider.

Before going out to the garden, we can hang the kettle over the hearth, adding a fresh log to catch the ebbing fire. Lamb or veal stew or boiled dinner will simmer all morning, and be ready by the time the family assembles, hungrier than a wolf pack. And at suppertime, steak, or hamburgers, or golden fried onions cook comfortably on the hearth.

Late evening brings a roasted apple on the fork, popcorn in the long-handled popper, mulled cider, hot in the old jug.

Roast corn, potatoes baked in the ashes — these are good too. In fact, there are so many things to cook in the fireplace that the electric range stands idle these autumn months except for coffee and regular baking.

The fireplace ministers to the family practically and spiritually, also. Nothing cheers the lonely heart more than the swift leap of flame up the old chimney.

The most beautiful fireplace I know is in an old stone house at Guilford. The house itself is enchanting — solid stone walls built long ago when the ferny forest was close and unspoiled.

Downstairs are two fireplaces, so wide that horses were used to drag the logs in. In these cramped days one could set up housekeeping in one such fireplace. Great dark beams support the weight above, and the stone hearths are wide enough for everyone. High-backed settles keep the cold air away, and the flame blazes warm and comforting.

Being of a romantic disposition, I can imagine a hunter just in from a faraway journey to Ticonderoga, walking soft and quick to the fire and speaking to the girl at the spinning wheel, dove-quiet in her gray gown, and with the firelight on her golden hair.

I wish I could have been there — and for all I know, maybe I was — when they had Thanksgiving. There were venison, wild turkey and maize; there were Indian potatoes, small and sweet; there were long loaves of crusty hot bread. Maybe they had spiced wild grape jelly, dark as amethyst and quivering with sweetness. They had mince pies and pumpkin pies, rich and spicy.

And the minister blessed the food. I like to think that he forgot, on that day, that we were all born in sin, that God was a terrible punishing deity. Warmed by the fire in those magnificent fire-places, and seeing the look of love in the eyes of the girl in the quiet gray gown, I am sure he felt God's goodness, and gave thanks for a life that was full, and for the simple kindness of man.

Now, so long away from those times, I think of our forefathers as Thanksgiving comes again. Their lives were hard and filled with struggle. Death walked in the dark woods and the Indians were always unknown quantities. They had no real ease in living, no luxuries. Out of a harsh wilderness they won themselves a great hearth, a life-giving fire, and the right to worship God as they pleased. And they were thankful.

When winter came to them, in those early days, it was a battle to survive. Those deep-drifting snows, the long dark night, the scarcity of food, the illness for which they had no cure; all these they faced. And yet at Thanksgiving they were glad. Thankful for the strings of apples dried against the wall; for the pumpkin hanging in sunny-yellow slices; for the butter packed in crocks and covered with home-rendered fat to preserve it; for the dried venison and the jars of parched corn.

We would do well in a world like ours, to go back to the simple thankfulness for the things that make a family life possible. I am thankful for the things we still have, despite the atom bomb. The terrible ingenuity of man may wipe us out in time to come. But now, on Thanksgiving, we still have the November sun, and the clear deep blue of the sky, and the white glory of the stars, and the loving-kindness of friends, just as our forefathers had. If only we can preserve the real things — the love of man and woman, the peace of an evening by the fire, the sweetness of music, and the gay sound of children's voices — we shall not have to hear the sound of the world disintegrating into chaos.

The last summer puppy rode away to his new home with almost the nicest people of the summer. The place seems empty, though, with only the old guard and a few extras. I wonder, if I never had to part with a puppy, whether the whole forty acres would, in time, be honeycombed with kennels and kennels, layer on layer. Yes, it would be lovely. But the kennels would all be empty, because all the dogs would undoubtedly be in the house.

In all the years of breeding spaniels, we have found that dog lovers are a good breed themselves. And they all speak the same language, whether they are cocker or French poodle or wirehair or Doberman fanciers. It is reassuring in this day and time so full of trouble and hate to find people who renew one's faith in humankind.

Only today we had dog-lover guests, a farmer and his wife and children. The family had started with almost no assets except themselves to make a farm provide them with a living. They had the land, an old house with no conveniences, and their own brave spirits.

The first year they lived almost entirely on what the man could shoot; and, he added, "I often think we lived better that year than any!" He said, "We had pheasant and quail most of the time."

He put out new apple trees, and worked over the old ones already on the land. His wife carried water by hand, used kerosene lamps, made apple jelly and butter, took care of babies. Meanwhile they worked toward the dream.

Now, after some years, the dream is being realized. They brought us two great baskets of apples — Duchess County, Golden Delicious, and Red Delicious; perfect, and firm, and crisp, and sweet. All the neighbors told him not to bother with Golden Delicious — they were too delicate and fussy. So he went ahead, and he nursed them along, invented a box to pack them in that wouldn't bruise them, and offered luxury fruit to the market. He has lived to see freight-car loads of fruit rot unsold, while his own perfect, hand-raised apples sold as fast as delivered. And all the time he keeps learning, reading, studying, watching the trees, testing this and that, and working.

And I sat there with happiness in my heart. I thought, "Thank God I am American! Pioneer courage still persists, we have our heritage, we are worth saving. We, the people, the ordinary American people, we shall build, not tear down civilization!" I felt humble and grateful for the friendship of the apple man who renewed my belief in humanity. What could I give them in return? Only my feeling for them, my respect, my admiration. I could know in my mind the lean days, the aching nights they had spent. I could feel the untimely hail-storms that ruined the crops, the blight, the long, hard days of picking.

But happy is he, and blessed is he who builds success out of himself. Yes, they started on forty dollars, but they just weren't forty dollar people. They took what they had, and went ahead and got results. "Someday we'll get plumbing," said the wife contentedly, "and I'm going to fix up the house. It's old."

They got in the ancient car and drove away in the twilight, and I watched them go. I was uplifted, yet a little sad all at once, because maybe I haven't realized every possibility myself. "I'll do better," I resolved, going in to start supper.

This year I cannot bear to see the leaves go. Early in the morning when I cross the frosty grass to let the spaniels out, I smell the leaves. I never noticed before how sweet they smell on autumn mornings. It's the kind of odor that quickens the heart, a clean, bright-bladed smell.

The cockers rush out, paws damp, hair ruffled, and they all roll and scuffle in the fallen oak and maple leaves. Only a few oak leaves are down; the oak keeps a dark, steady red against the sky long after the other trees are bare. Even the remote Honey feels the spell, and today she came pacing along the terrace carrying an empty meat can in her mouth, of all things. Head up, tail going, she pranced, positively pranced.

All at once I felt guilty. I could see

how she would look hunting pheasants, golden in the tawny thickets and carrying a brilliant bird. Mentally I apologized to all the dogs for denying them their birthright. Even now, I thought, I would take up hunting — but what would I do if we killed something? Then Honey ran past me and looked at me over the meat tin, her eyes full of mischief. She was just having fun, she said, flipping her tail briskly.

I like the rugged vegetables, cabbage and parsnips and carrots; and as for a good acorn squash, baked with butter and salt and pepper, possibly stuffed with sausage, I'd turn up my nose at squab for it any minute.

My nephew Don's crop of pumpkins was a pleasant surprise. They were destined to be jack-o'-lanterns, but we could have illuminated the whole state of Connecticut if we had used them all. So we tried chopping them in pieces and steaming them, and then not making pies but mashing them with salt and pepper and butter. They were young and tender and flavor-perfect.

My passion for the rugged vegetables

is not shared by either my child, Cicely, or by Jill's two. They feel it would be a far, far better world if squash had never been discovered as edible. So far as they are concerned it isn't. They will eat sweet corn until they are completely buried in bare cobs. The end of the sweet corn season is a sad, sad time. When ours is positively gone, to the last drying nubbin, they want to find somebody who still has some. The hunt grows feverish as the stalks wither. Finally Cicely will sigh and say, "Mother, why don't we really plant some corn next year? I mean so we can have enough!"

"We can't put the whole forty acres in corn," I answer.

"I don't see why not!"

"Who's going to hoe it?"

That quiets her. We have never been able to persuade the children that gardening is an invigorating, refreshing, gay sport.

Our yard has taken on its customary winter look. I have read several articles in my favorite magazines about winter landscaping. Ours is in a class by itself. All over the place stand large bulky affairs caparisoned richly in burlap, bearing the legend, "Stillmeadow, Southbury, Conn." An orange onion sack makes a spot of color in the back, wrapping the trunk of Jill's Seckel pear. The holly, which by rights ought to be a winter decoration, is completely buried in oak leaves, and tied up in old grain sacks. Old dog food cartons, pegged down with assorted slats, cover the small perennials. Chicken wire waistcoats guard the young stripling trees. But the most striking objet d'art is the black fig tree, perilously clad in a kind of Taj Mahal of wood, gunnysacking, and clothesline.

Our winter landscaping is different, at least. Nobody has anything like it anywhere in this part of New England.

There is nothing stingy about New England rains. Along about this time of year we begin to say things like, "Better scrub the kennels while it's so nice and sunny." I look out the window and see a small rabbit of cloud hopping over the hill and say feverishly, "I think I'll wash the blankets right away. One last time."

Then it rains. The first day I attempt

33

to ignore it. The fury of water sluicing over the house. The shut-down sky. The general limpness of everything outside. I can't seem to get organized for any work. I keep thinking, "I'll wait until it clears up." The second day I tell myself it is good for the subsoil. The evergreens will like it. Maybe the garden will be better next summer. Yes, maybe. But by now there is water in the cellar, and the furnace isn't better for that, nor the water heater, nor yet my lovely jars of food. Upstairs the woodwork feels damp.

We keep the fireplaces roaring. Of course, the woodshed is not full, and the only dry wood we have is in that woodshed. By night of the second day we put the logs on sparingly. Esmé sits practically in the fire. The dogs quite sensibly sleep and sleep. At night the wind changes and it rains harder. I snap at the family. I am irritated at the cockers for being able to sleep that way. If they sleep all night, how can they sleep all day too?

By the third day, usually, the wood gives out. This makes everything just dandy. We sally forth for logs that look as though they were brought up from the bottom of the sea, and burn equally well. Even the cannel coal for the front fireplace is getting low. There is water on the window sills. The icebox looks as if a fire sale had been going on in it. In short, there is nothing good in anything.

I finally decide to go out for some shingles to revive the fire, and I get out last year's ski pants. I can't get them around my middle this year! No amount of breathing in, or pushing, or struggling will get me inside those pants. The awful implications in this literally drive me distracted. It is the zero hour.

Then the next morning, when I wake up and look out, I see it is raining even harder. It isn't possible, but it's true. As I watch the long lines of water fling themselves at the soaked world, all at once I feel a reluctant kind of admiration creeping over me. Nature is nothing if not thorough, I think. An all-or-nothing girl. It is dramatic the way this rain builds up and builds up. The weather is so foul it is beginning to be exciting.

I climb into my old corduroys, wrap up my head, and go right on out. I suppose I feel vaguely the way Alpine guides feel as they pick out a nice slippery glacier and mount it. The rain soaks right through everything, and the yard is a running swamp. Go on, see if I care! I slosh down the road for the mail, feeling like those people you see in the news reels doing things in tanks under water.

At the top of the road I can see Stillmeadow behind me. My favorite legend is the story of Lyonnesse, the little village that sank beneath the waves and rises again at Christmas for one night, and the church bell rings over the sea, and the villagers go to the little church and pray, and at dawn the village sinks again. Well, the house looks like a house in Lyonnesse.

And it is very beautiful just because the rain is so intense. The world is nothing but water. The postman drives up and reaches the mail out with a long arm. His eyes smile, his wise Yankee face is framed in rain. Water swishes down the hood of his car.

"How long will this keep up?" I ask. "You think it might clear up tomorrow?"

"Well," he says, "might, and might not."

I feel perfectly content as I wade home. I also feel perfectly sure he knows just what the weather will be. But he won't commit himself. I respect the fact.

There is, of course, a good deal of pure tripe written about us Yankees. As a reclaimed Yankee, I can count myself in on it. It was only an accident that I was born in Colorado, and lived all over the country half my life, South, West, Middlewest and New York — which is a very special locale. It gives me a good deal of pleasure to recognize many of my traits as pure, unadulterated Yankee. Close-mouthed. Mind your own business and never rush in and try to push people around your way. Never talk big about tomorrow's eggs.

Washed back into the house, I am giggling about a nice exhibition of it last week when, at a neighborhood party, one man asked another if he got his shaves in Woodbury. There was a full five-minute silence. Finally, having revolved the whole question pro and con, the second man delivered his answer.

"Well," he said slowly, "no."

I found an antidote one year, however. I gave myself one of those rainy days as a vacation. And I can heartily recommend the procedure. Rain was a silver sheet on the window when I woke up. The sky was like a gray lake upside down over the house. "All right," I said, "I am just going to take the whole day off."

I turned on Don Goddard, my favorite news announcer, and put my breakfast on a tray. I made pancakes and put both butter and maple sirup on them. No thin tomato juice and black coffee this day. I got back in bed and ate my lovely fattening pancakes and read a new magazine. I felt much better about the weather.

The rest of the day I did all the things I like to do and none of the things I hate. I wrote some special letters, not in a hurry, but taking time to really visit with the friends I wrote to. I polished my silver mirror, which I never get time to do; I played a long time with Melody and Silver and Hildegarde, and brushed all the others.

I listened to a Burl Ives album of folk songs and the César Franck symphony. By noon I was feeling decidedly mellow, and the incessant rain looked rather pleasant outside. The house was, after all, nice and cozy. So for lunch I had chili con carne with tamales simmered on top and dark rye bread (without seeds). I read some poetry and the newest who-dunnit. I made some fresh hot ginger-bread. By the time the family got home for dinner I was the sunniest person I ever saw.

And then, after dinner, the rain slackened and stopped and a pale lovely light spread over a clean sky and the world was almost too beautiful to endure. "Well," I thought, "we do have to have rainy spells or we never would have this incredible loveliness. The lesson is plain." The fallen leaves shone in the light with a faint luster, the eaves dripped silver. Honey came in shaking golden drops from her damp fur. And just at the very last moment before night, a single flash of sun lighted the horizon, a pure breathless gold.

Jill is pruning the berry bushes and grapevines and young trees, which she didn't have time to do before. We are cleaning the long flower border and digging parsnips. We have found parsnips keep best for us just tossed in a pile, covered with earth and leaves, and a bushel basket turned over them. We dig them out as they are needed.

We have good success growing endive in a box of damp sand in the cellar. We cover the crowns with five or six inches of sand, or sand mixed half and half with soil. Nothing is more delicious than cool, crisp endive long after the garden salads have gone.

We visited a man in Old Greenwich last week who has a cold frame in which he keeps all his winter vegetables. We are going to build a frame as soon as we can, and do the same. He puts cabbage, carrots, celery, beets and turnips in the frame, then covers the vegetables thoroughly with dry oak leaves. He says oak leaves stay drier than any other leaf. On sunny days he props the frame partly open, and on damp, cold days he keeps it closed. He has crisp vegetables the year around.

Esmé's fur begins to darken now that winter is coming. Tigger will lose his summer leaness and his black body will be plump and gleaming again. I don't know whether the theory is correct that cats are thin in summer because they eat bugs. So far as has been known, Esmé's aristocratic little mouth has never opened for a bug, but she too is thin in summer. She brought a small mouse to the door last week and sang out loudly to be admired, then she laid it down and came in to eat her own food, a dish of egg and milk. A Siamese cat eats so daintily with tiny lap-laps, not a hair of her narrow jaw wet. She finishes her meal, then leaps from table to chest looking for a bowl of flowers to drink from. Tigger, on the other hand, lays to with a hearty will and drinks lustily from the regular watering bowl.

Tigger is always overcome by love as soon as I sit down at the typewriter. He pushes himself under my arm and purrs like a motorboat. My lap is full of black cat, and I type around ears and whiskers while he turns his large eyes on me with a bland look. If Top-Hat, the black cocker puppy, sees him, he bounces up and down, cocker-wise, to signify that I should take him up, too. He is jealous of the cats and they of him, but they play together just the same, so long as it is not a question of my lap.

There is an elusive quality about

November sunlight. The Connecticut hills are beautiful with a special beauty. At night, little faraway houses, never seen in summer, suddenly prick the dark with their lamps. Fields of winter wheat appear, visible now the leaves are down. All the browns, a thousand browns, come out. Rust-brown, sand-brown, topaz-brown, and the faded gold of harvest fields. The contour of the land is evident, folds and hills and valleys. The sky over all is soft and hazy, and there is a feeling in the air that winter is coming. The shadows look different, sloping across the pale grass. This is a peaceful, serene land, and never quite so peaceful as now, with the crops in, wood piled high, houses snugged down, brooks running slow with leaves. The days grow shorter. Dusk comes before we are finished with the day.

But we had one last picnic at Eight Mile last Sunday night. We carried the charcoal grill and broiled bacon and hamburgers and drank hot coffee. The sun went down in a blaze of apricot light and the water was dark and still.

My heart got to aching for all the sad people all over the world. I wanted so terribly to share the color and the peace and the serene fall of evening and the clean cold air coming up from the water. And I wanted families together, going quietly home at night. This, I thought, is what we must have in this world again, somehow. Not power and glory, not magnificence. Only freedom for folk to work and be at peace in their own lands.

The baskets were loaded back in the car, and Don gave up casting for the unattainable pickerel. "I almost had a strike," he murmured.

The house was warm and inviting when we got home, and smelled of bayberry and burning apple wood. And white moonlight began to sift through the windows. This time of year has much comfort in it, when all is said and done.

Thanksgiving this year should be a holiday filled with thankfulness to God that our American way of life has been preserved. America is certainly far from perfect, but it is still a country founded on faith in God instead of faith in a dictator. It is a good country, wide and spacious and with fertile valleys and tall blue mountains. It is a homeland where our children and our children's children should grow up without fear, walking with their heads high and their eyes clear and serene.

In the years ahead we have much to do. It is easy to lose sight of the important things. There will be many new inventions; money will buy undreamed of gadgets; we shall want more and better mousetraps than ever before. I am afraid of this. Happiness is not upholstered in velvet, nor lighted by the push of a button. If we start a new wild scramble for material luxury, we shall begin a toboggan slide to destruction. I do believe in pleasant living, as much as our means afford — but I wish we could chart a modest course between overelegance and simplicity.

The happiest homes I have known I can describe very well, though I cannot remember the fabrics or decorations in them. I remember them for a sort of glow, a radiance over everything; and it was not indirect illumination, it was the glow of a warm and happy spirit inhabiting the home.

As for the actual physical components of a home, they can be very simple. It is how they are put together that gives them charm. Color, for instance, is not expensive. A room can be warm with daffodil yellow, or cool and quiet with apple green, or poetic with blue, whether the curtains be cotton or satin. Ten-cent candles are beautiful, and candle-light is glamorous. It is much better, it seems to me, to make something of what we have and can afford, than to yearn for something more expensive and fashionable.

Almost anyone can have flowers. In the city the pushcarts have small bouquets that are inexpensive, and in the city or country there is always green to be had, many kinds of shining green leaves. In the country the wild flowers are beautiful if you have no garden. From the first white violet to Queen Anne's lace and goldenrod, there is a succession planting better than man can devise. I am always enchanted to see how the colors change with the changing seasons, the brilliant yellows and ambers and russets and the blues of late fall softening into the sober gold of the last roadside flowers. Midsummer has the pinks and reds, the roses and clarkia and all the sturdy annuals. Spring has the apple-blossom tints and the spring blue of violets and blue-eyed Marys. They all have their own beauty.

The enchantment of a November evening has in it the feeling of pumpkins and squash in glowing heaps, of crops harvested, woodpiles trim, cedar boughs piled around drafty house sills. The fields are beautiful as they give themselves over to night. All the tawny shades, the coppery tones, the ambers and rusts are incredibly lovely. You can see these colors now that lush summer and lavish autumn are flowing to winter. The delicate shades of color emerge until every dead weed stalk is a different tone.

As I walked down the road I could see much farther than before, with the branches no longer bearing the flood tide of leafage. Distant hills and the roll of the meadow, and the separate stone fences. The last feather of light made an enchantment. I thought of Keats: "How tiptoe Night holds back her dark grey hood."

"Season of mists and mellow fruitfulness" — this was it. There was a mist on the swamp, where the blueberry bushes still had a faint garnet tone.

Honey started a rabbit, but nothing came of it. We were both satisfied. She came back and moved demurely by me as though she personally would have no traffic with rabbits anyway. I picked a cinnamon-colored stick and bit the dry end and then wondered if any poison ivy had grown anywhere near it. It doesn't pay for me to be so poetic that I forget poison ivy.

I turned and walked back with the cold sweet air in my face. No matter what men do, the late fall stars come out the same to move the heart with beauty. The earth keeps her seasons. Sun and wind and rain are vouchsafed humanity. Nothing can take away the security we have in the earth herself. And no mad dictators can lift their iron gloves and wipe off that delicate lilac color above the dark hill. The earth endures, her strength restores us.

I opened the picket gate, which is now so badly in need of painting, and walked over the mole-gutted lawn with Honey preceding me. It had come to her that it was probably past suppertime, and there might be leftover turkey soup around.

She would accept a dish of turkey soup, and she made with considerable briskness for the kitchen door.

I took a last look at the sky above the great maples. The sky and the maples and the darkness made the house seem very small. The house belongs to us, and we are allowed to work on the earth around it. The earth is bigger, the sky and stars and moon and sun are too big to belong to man.

Thankful I was for the enduring things, and that I, such a small finite creature, have been allowed to recognize the beauty of the world in my small and finite way. The planes that blot the stars from view are soon gone, and there are the stars again, serene.

December

Song for December

The snow invades the land, silent and deep,
Levels the meadows, blurs the darkened
   hill,
And Christmas candles burn where good
   folk keep
A welcome light for him who brings
   goodwill.

Across the centuries, in alien land,
Once wise men knelt and dreamed of
   kingdoms won —
Unsceptered still the Christ-child's open
   hand,
Yet they perceived great destiny begun.

Bitter the fare of our atomic day,
Diminished now the glory of their dream,
For many things for which we used to pray
Now most unlikely and illusive seem.

Yet where the Christmas candles shed their
   light,
Behold how kind the face of Christ tonight!

LIVING IN THE country in winter is not easy. It is not simply sitting by a log fire and reading that good book. It is no life for lazy people. One morning always comes when you are snowed in, no matter whether you planned to go out or not. You can't even open the front door.

You have to shovel to get to the kennel, and shoveling snow is just like tossing up spadefuls of cement. The road crew gets held up somewhere along the line, and of course the telephone wires are down.

If there is a real blizzard sweeping down from the ice palace of the old king of winter, the next thing is that "the electric," as we call it in these parts, is cut off. And when the electric is off, so goes the furnace, the water pump, the freezer and the stove.

But for us country life continues to be wonderful. Nothing in the city compares, as far as I am concerned, with the sight of George plunging through hip-deep drifts, his shovel on his shoulder. "Guess you need a little help," he says. I rest on my shovel, and watch the swift easy rhythm of his arms as the snow rolls back like the waters of the sea in the Old Testament.

Then there is the excitement of the arrival of the light-and-power men. Everyone bundles up and goes out to watch as they climb up ice-encased poles, and patch up the interrupted life-current for our equipment.

We pile up logs in the old fireplace; and if there is anything a city-dweller can have half as pleasant as a filled woodshed, I know not what it would be. We hang the iron kettle over the flame, and the good smell of onion, salt pork, and potatoes fills the room. If the electric is off some time we can get our meals in the fireplace or on the old range in the back kitchen. And candlelight is nice.

Then finally the lights go on and the hum of the furnace can be heard, and we feel as if we had bested winter again. It is a fine feeling.

When the first snow arrives, I really give myself up to winter. The air comes cold and sharp and there is a quickening in the blood, a feeling that the seasons are rolling around quite the way they should, and all is well. Snow has fallen heavily for two days. In the country the dogs are happy. They roll in it, they gulp great mouthfuls, they shake their fur ecstatically, they race up and down and around the house.

In the city the street-cleaning department looks on snow as a crisis. There is always a terrible to-do over snow in New York. One would think New York was a tropical city, and snow an unheard-of phenomenon. Generally, before the snow is carted away there are various battles. The head of one department accuses the head of another department of inefficiency. Taxpayers write in to the papers about their streets. The mayor issues orders to car owners. The taxis never have chains; they skid into one another and the drivers get out and shout furiously. The snow is loaded in trucks with machines like hay loaders. Finally, as the last load roars away, the weather turns warm and it rains.

We shovel the paths at Stillmeadow with an old broken coal shovel. Or else we flounder from drift to drift in careless fashion. Nature in the raw is easier to take in the country — perhaps that is it.

Star has just come in with ice-balls between her toes. She wants them all taken out, and she says so quite plainly. Ronnie looks like a black sleek seal against the white bank of snow. Sunbonnet has snow on her absurdly long black lashes. But Honey, of course, stays quite dry, even in the snow. A few flakes may lie on her tawny coat, but she shakes them off and walks dry-footed to the fire. Little Pussy flies through the air like a swift dark bird. The earth will hardly hold that one, with her wild shy spirit. Sometimes I think the two pussies are only mortal because they love their humans.

Spring Night and Seductive both quiver with ecstasy when they are held, but there's a faraway look in their eyes just the same. Big Pussy grows a bush of fur in winter; it makes her face look a bit like a baby panda's.

"Do they really understand what you say to them?" asked a non-doggy guest. "You just talk to them like people."

"Every single word," I assured her.

I am constantly amazed at their understanding. They do respond to every word — or to the tone quality of the word, which is more important. Perhaps they wouldn't get so much if they were spoken to in a monotone. But the only limit to their understanding is the range and color of my own voice. Everything I can express they respond to. If I tell them something exciting is going to happen, they are wild with excitement. They prance, throw balls in the air, skip around the furniture, jump all over me, and their tails spin like tops. The littlest puppy will listen as I say, "Oh, why didn't you use the paper?" and then fly to me to be comforted for his own mistake. "Who's my own darling Honey?" brings on an attack of devotion from even the remote and beautiful one.

Ronnie talks back. He murmurs under his breath, interspersing his remarks with long sighs. Meanwhile he lies upside down in my arms, and when I stop rubbing his stomach he lifts a paw and taps me, much after the manner of Grandma Star.

"Go on," the paw insists, "go on. I like this."

Sister and Honey came to town with us this time, and a very odd pair they make. Sister is such a stable, self-reliant little piece and she loves town life. In the back of her mind is the smug satisfaction that she is in New York and Star is in the country because she, Sister, does not bite strangers.

Sister floats along on the leash, light as a butterfly, so I keep peering around to be sure she is still there. Honey walks with her head over her shoulder, looking backward, as if something would get her from behind if she relaxed a moment. She starts nervously when a truck roars by, bucks suddenly at a dragon bus.

I was explaining this to Jill. I had been down Manhattan Avenue, which is a very quiet dead-end street.

Jill said, reasonably, "But there isn't any traffic there."

"No, but the houses look funny," I said. "You know there's always something funny."

You wouldn't think a cocker spaniel would be sensitive to architecture, would you? Well, Honey peered distrustfully at the old brownstone houses, the dark, peeling stone steps, the odd embrasures. It wasn't, she averred, natural. It made a dog uneasy; no knowing what you might find next. Once we came to a cleaning outfit, a machine blasting a stone front. Honey flew through the air — without a flying trapeze, too — her eyes starting from her head. Then she saw Sister quietly heeling along, looking dreamy and content, and suddenly Honey rushed wildly to her and kissed her face and fell into line beside her. Sister was a lifeboat in a stormy sea. Sister gave me a look from a wise bright eye, as one should say, "Well, after all, she's related to Star, and you know that black bitch . . ."

Honey is very fond of milk. This is a highly individual taste; some of our dogs won't touch it. Sister won't eat chopped beef unless it's cooked. Neither of them likes bones, but Windy, Star, and Ronnie would die for any old bone.

Sister always begins her meal by an indifferent approach to the bowl. She tries to bury it. If there isn't a newspaper around to tear up and use, she hopefully scrubs her nose along the bare boards, rushes the bowl, pushes it, scrapes the floor again. After this has gone on for five minutes, she begins to eat busily. The burying is just part of the ritual, like unfolding a napkin. But Sister is a conventional soul, and if this is proper, she's going to do it. Meanwhile Honey, who wouldn't know a convention when she smelled it, tries to gobble her supper fast enough to eat Sister's too.

We have been snowed in for some days after the blizzard that roared in from all directions. When it begins to snow all ways at once, I urge my husband to bring in more wood. Invariably he says it is just a flurry. I have known Bob to stick his head out and nearly have it snapped off with swirling sleet and say happily, "It's letting up; I don't think it will last much longer."

Wind and snow and sleet made a white darkness everywhere. I could hardly see the barn from the house; snow piled against doors and windows until they wouldn't open. All night long wild stallions of storm pounded past. When it finally cleared the drifts were dazzling silver. Under ice-smooth crust the snow was deep and heavy. The sun was white-gold and the sky as pure and serene as lake water. The shadows were cobalt on the snow.

Jill improved the indoor hours by varnishing the kitchen and bathroom linoleum with a new clear varnish that actually dries in somewhere near the time it is supposed to. She finished with a coat of paste wax, put on by hand and knee. Of course, the cats walked on it before the varnish was dry. Esmé was vastly curious and leaped to the middle to see what this was all about. "Oh, mercy," she said in good Siamese. She got out, lifting and shaking each paw as it was raised. This gave her an odd, stiff-legged, jerking progress like a marionette.

Then Tigger moved his large black bulk out, and when he found that sticky stuff on his feet, he sat right down where he was to wash it off.

Being snowbound gives time to play a mort of records. We go all the way from Marian Anderson singing Brahms songs from Opus 91, to the Gershwin album. Gilbert and Sullivan are excellent for a gray, snowy day. There are times in winter when César Franck or Beethoven would inspire me to dig into a snowdrift and stay there. Or Sibelius. More cheering to sing along with, "Never mind the why or wherefore, Love can level ranks and therefore, Though his Lordship's station's mighty, Though stupendous be his brain —"

Cicely's large collection of folk music makes a whole evening. The cockers enjoy the music too. Snow lies on two pillows, her head on the higher one. Clover and Sister are draped over each other; Honey lies on the floor, facing the cabinet. If there is any whistling in a record, the whole gang rises and barks madly, and rushes about.

It is a good thing to read a few lines of poetry before going to bed, in between letting cats in and dogs out. This winter I mean to reread also such books as *Walden* and the letters of Keats, and *Wuthering Heights*, and all of Katherine Mansfield — I can't read her often enough.

I wish Katherine Mansfield could be a visitor at Stillmeadow. She would feel the beauty of every small branch; she would understand Esmé. Probably our cockers would be too vigorous for her, except for the remote Honey. I would have her tea absolutely boiling. Imagine sitting by the fire with Katherine Mansfield, while her bright delicate wit enchanted the household.

Sometimes I play a game with myself on these snow-deep days when even the mailman comes only as far as the corner. I choose an imaginary companion, and how real and close they come. My friends range from Charlotte Brontë to Keats. I'd love to have Emily, but she wouldn't come. Charlotte is easier, though shy and retiring. Keats goes right down to the fruit cellar to see the "lucent syrops tinct with cinnamon," the jams and jellies. Keats had such a zest for life, a rich and deep perception of beauty.

I don't feel so much at home with Shelley. Any minute he might turn that dazzling gaze on me and say, "Let's try the great adventure now," and set the house on fire. He was slightly notional. Byron I admit I would rather meet at someone else's house. But Byron would be horribly bored with me. Not being dark or slim or beautiful, never being able to "walk in beauty like the night," I wouldn't get any attention from Byron

61

and I wouldn't have the kind of small talk to carry it off.

Now, in the deep heart of winter, the heart turns in on itself for content. Imaginary companions, music, poetry, whatever the wind cannot assail nor the snow bury, have their season. If you are really isolated, as we are so much of this month, you dig down into your own resources.

My very best Oriental in the living room has lost most of its fringe, and the edges are scalloped. Star's first litter was born on it. She didn't like her box. The babies grew up digging at the rug, chewing it, wetting on it. Now I like that old rug better than any new one. Those were our first cocker babies, and I was so incredibly happy. I like to look at the old rug and see in memory those puppies tumbling across the pattern and wobbling up to me with their mouths full of fringe.

When a visiting friend said in distress, "Oh, why don't you put down a grass rug and save this?" I asked, "Save it for what? I'm living here now."

I don't believe in saving things for some future that may not come. Things laid away and saved so often are not used by anyone. The world is too uncertain. I believe deeply that we should live with as much beauty as we can, every single day that we live. We should surround our daily life with as much charm and graciousness as we possibly can. I had rather my child look back and say, "I remember mother used a filet cloth and ivory candles and the old silver," than for her to dig around in an attic and say, "Look at the moth-eaten junk in here. Let's sell it."

The only heritage we can be sure of passing on is a lovely memory. Very often I am saddened to think that Cicely can never have as glowing memories of me as I have of my own mother, who made every day a gracious and charming thing. I must try, I think, to subdue my sinus, and be more patient with the electric company.

In a world of change and confusion we need Christmas more than ever. For me it is the time when my mother seems closest to me, and that shows in itself what the time is. The years between seem to slip away on Christmas Eve, and I really sense her continued presence.

Easter may be supposed to be the time for a renewal of faith in immortality, but for me it is Christmas. It isn't the burgeoning of spring that contents my soul, but the clear starlight of a December night. The feeling that Christmas has always been and will always be, and that the spirit of man will rise above any indignity offered it — somehow this feeling really comforts and sustains me.

Memory is one of the most mysterious gifts of God. Some moment will remain as long as we live, some hours vanish like foam on a wave crest.

Some things I remember are important, and some just seem to be there for no good reason. The breathless ecstasy of the first real date, the first dance, and the first kiss — anybody would remember these. But I remember when my best friend read about a wonderful hair tint, and tried it, and came to school the next day with her head green.

I dare say most people have the same odd assortment tucked in their minds.

Another peculiar thing about memory — at least mine — is that I can remember exactly how every pin tray was on my mother's dresser, and yet I have no recollection of where I put this month's coal bill. I can close my eyes and see the little red velvet pincushion, the hairpin tray with roses on it, the hair receiver, without which no dresser was then complete, and a lovely hatpin container. I can see mother's face in the mirror, dark brown hair pinned under a real-hair net, straight nose dusted with talcum. She always looked young and beautiful to me, even though I knew parents were terribly, terribly old.

I don't believe any poet has written so perfect an expression of the way one remembers a small thing out of the midst of a great emotion as Rossetti. "The Woodspurge" is one of my favorites of his lyrics.

"My eyes wide open, had the run
  Of some ten weeds to fix upon;
  Among those few, out of the sun,
  The woodspurge flowered, three
   cups in one.
  From perfect grief there need not
   be
  Wisdom or even memory.

One thing then learnt remains to
  me:
The woodspurge has a cup of
  three."

I don't think many things in this world
are so soul-warming as doing over your
own furniture. Working with wood is
delightful; wood has a good feel to it,
and old wood in old furniture carries all
the extra satisfaction of renewing lost
loveliness by your own labor. The maple
chair recalls a bygone day when some
real artist carved it and shaped the curve
of the legs. What crinoline skirts were
spread over it, what bombazine settled
stiffly in it? And then from what long
decline from glory it suffered until it
acquired a mask of white paint and stood
in some kitchen or on a porch as "that
old chair from grandfather's dining
room." And now, glowing again, it lives
in Stillmeadow, loved and cherished
among the other reclaimed old pieces.

We have only one antique I wish we
could get rid of, and that is the washing
machine. The very next windfall we
have, I hope, will drop a nice new model
in the back kitchen. The old one has

washed all the clothes it ought to. Washing has grown to be quite an adventure. For one thing, the machine shudders and makes odd noises. The wringer changes its mind right in the middle of a sheet, and rushes backward at a terrific speed. Sometimes it chews bits out of silk pajamas in some mysterious fashion.

I spend long hours poring over the magazines, looking doubtfully at the slim, elegant girls who are doing the wash with one gloved hand while they go to a bridge game and deal cards with the other. I don't think even an advertiser could do a Stillmeadow washing without a backward glance. All I really ask for is a washer with a cheerful disposition and a progressive attitude toward too many sheets in at once. And one that doesn't make queer noises and bite the clothes.

I do, myself, love to wash. When I get very, very low in my mind, or suffer some special grief, the job of doing the wash is an easement. I run over the house and catch up a tubful of something and wash. I like the clean, good smell of soap and the steam from the hot water faucet. And the feeling of working at something tangible is good. Clothes blowing in the wind and sun, clean and sweet. "You see," I tell myself, "there is always some small work to do, the world goes on, and the simple ordinary things of life are good."

I sometimes wonder what women do who never can work at a simple, humble physical task when they are sad. What do they do in the Waldorf-Astoria when life hurts them?

Christmas is almost upon us before we get over Thanksgiving. Many simple folk like me are thinking long thoughts this Christmas as we wrap the packages. We are still waiting for peace. We are insecure, when we have won the war. Civil conflicts exist everywhere, peoples are still starving, Labor and Management are embroiled in half the world. Nations still argue unsolved issues. Race prejudice snakes along every hidden byway.

This must not be. The aggressive instincts have run the world into destruction, culminating in the desperate promise of the atomic bomb that man shall perish from the earth, and the earth from the cosmos.

What is the answer for us? The creative instincts, the love force must be nourished with every beat of our hearts until they overbalance the destructive instincts. And this cannot be accomplished by any great legislation. It will be the sum of the little people's feeling. Good will toward men, that is the answer. Every mother and every father has the future life of the world in control. We have got to stop lining up as Fascists, Communists, Laborites, Gentiles, Jews, Negroes and Whites. Somehow, by some divine light, we have got to see ourselves as people, one and all.

Our children learn from us. This is a solemn and terrible responsibility. They learn from what we say and from what we do not say. The Nazi children who sent their parents to concentration camps had learned one way of life. We must have our children learn a better one. Parents who say, "I don't like Jews," are the very parents who are trying to raise their children in the Christian ideal. They should be saying, "Jesus was a Jew."

But I believe on this Christmas, this very special and holy Christmas, that we must have a faith in all the human beings of tomorrow; that we must look at life somehow steadily and whole, and not destroy ourselves and our children's children with hate. I do not believe the men we have lost have died in vain; I shall never believe it. If humanity was destined to be pulverized by atomic energy, there would never have been a Jesus, born so long ago in that darkling stable.

The Christmas presents are stacked under the tree on Christmas Eve. And the best-loved are not the most expensive, but the ones that make you feel the giver just knew what you liked! Home-made are the dearest; they involve effort and thought. The best one of my whole childhood was the doll's house my father built all himself, a magnificent edifice with a front porch and railing, an elevator, and a fireplace in the parlor. Every room had different wallpaper, and there were carpets from wall to wall. That was a long time ago, the doll house gone the way of all things; but in my memory it is still flawless. The tiny baby rocks forever in the pink, lacy bassinet.

And the mother, dressed in black lace, stands forever in the parlor on a bright green carpet!

Now a Christmas gift is exactly as timeless and enchanted as loving thoughts make it. One of my best gifts last Christmas was a wreath made by hand, on a wire hanger, from Connecticut evergreens. I came back from a trip to New York, tired, and anxious about all those things which pile up when a housewife goes away. One of those lovely, early snows had been falling for hours, and I drove through a kind of lacy twilight down the winter road. I saw my friend walking away from Stillmeadow along the shadowy path, and she waved and said she had been to the house. I drove on, and there was the house in the sweet twilight of snow, and on the door the Christmas wreath she had carried over and put up. Deep green of pine, cinnamon brown of cones, a spray of gay little bells, and a flash of rosy ribbon.

"This," I thought, "is what I mean by Christmas! To come home, after absence, and find the gracious thoughtfulness expressed, the good and gracious warmth of friendship."

I know there are people who come out even with their Christmas wrappings, but I am not one of them. I always run out of silver tying cord while I still have yards and yards of splendid paper left. Or I have so much ribbon that the cats play all over the house trailing it in clouds of glory while I search frantically for just one more bit of star paper for that last book. Sometimes I wonder if those sets of ready-matched wrappings would solve the problem, but in my heart I know they wouldn't. Because no two presents are the same size.

I always hope my friends will like my gifts as well as I do. I love things, pretty, fragile, colorful things. Buying the right present for someone is a heady and exhilarating joy.

The loveliest part of Christmas is often an unexpected remembrance. A box of gardenia sachet in white satin made me glow all day last year because it came from an admired and well-loved person.

My mother always said that she wanted to express her feelings about people while she and they were still alive. She sent many a little gift surreptitiously, and

72

bought many a small bunch of flowers for friends. "I don't believe in sending flowers to funerals," she said, with a lift of her fine, dark brows. "It's while we live we need flowers!"

When I think of my mother, I know how much she knew of gracious living, and wish that I, too, could have her fine quality of living like a gentle lady, warm, and wise, and generous. And I wish I could tell her, as the year rolls around, her daughter still tries to walk in the ways she trod, stumbling often, but very willing.

We have a family characteristic that we have always had. We often buy gifts and secrete them — and forget them. They turn up in odd places later in the year, and are greeted with pleased surprise. In fact, a pair of pajamas I bought for Cicely last Christmas turned up just in time to put under the tree this year! Any way you look at it, this adds an element of zest to closet-cleaning and drawer-straightening. Almost anything may turn up. And it is rather nice in August to discover a new manicure set labeled happily, MERRY CHRISTMAS.

There are two distinct schools of

thought about Christmas gifts. One school believes gifts must be luxuries, never anything you need. The other believe people should get what they actually and badly need. I veer wildly between the two schools. I indulge in a useless gadget like a box of sachet, and proceed to stockings and underwear. Books go to my head like strong drink, because books belong in both categories. Who could live without them?

As we get ready for Christmas I go over the jars in the fruit cellar, for I think homemade jams and jellies are fine gifts. I always make a little damson plum conserve and some extra chili sauce and garden special for friends who cannot put things up. Gifts of good food are welcome anywhere now.

The gifts I love most are those that make me think the giver has a personal feeling about me. I have two handmade dishcloths which I treasure because of the thought that went into them. But the loveliest gift I have had in a long time was not a Christmas gift.

I met a group of people at a neighbor's swimming pool one breathless August day. One woman wore a pair of flat disk earrings, and being an earring addict I couldn't help saying, "Oh, how beautiful your earrings are!"

Eight months later we had met frequently and become friends. And one day we were having a farewell class in flower arranging, when Ruth came up to me and said, "I have a little something I want you to have. Hold out your hand, and please don't object." I held out my hand and she put something in it, and when I looked, there were those earrings!

"This," I thought, "is what giving really means. All those months she remembered how much I admired them, and knew how pleased I would be to wear them." And I thought, "If all the world could get a small bit of this generosity, we should not worry about problems, for there would be none. What a happy world we should have!"

Loving-kindness is what we need. And it does not involve money; it involves the heart. So as I get ready for this Christmas season, I wish every woman could stop the fretting and rushing and buying, which is making inflation a monster to swallow us all, and simply sit down and think of what she has right in her home that someone would enjoy. If the gift says, "I cherish the thought of you, my friend," it is a fine gift.

Christmas we must keep. We must have a tree, and sing carols, and light the candle for the Christ child. For we are dedicated, in American life, to the preserving of certain ideals.

As we celebrate this year, we must resolve to keep our lives free from racial intolerance, from bigotry and hate. We must do everything we can to defeat cruelty in our own country.

I must think of these matters, and as we let the candlelight shine over new-fallen snow in our small spot of earth, I must remember the long centuries which have passed since this birth. I think of all the great and good men who have walked the earth, giving their strength and their lives for humanity. There have been enough of them to counterbalance these others — yes, there have been enough.

And surely Christmas is a time to rededicate ourselves to the good, the true, the beautiful. To remember our own dead under white crosses, and keep Christmas for them, too.

Carol-singing time is here. How glad I am that we live in a country where carols are still sung. I have been thinking so sadly of the poor German children who have lost "Stille Nacht, Heilige Nacht"; and for all I know, "O Tannenbaum" also. The German sounds so soft and clear in carols; but in martial, blood-thirsty tunes, I don't care for it. I hope the English never lose "Good King Wenceslas" or "God Rest You Merry, Gentlemen." This is almost my favorite; it seems to echo back to the days of Shakespeare. God rest you merry — that is a warm greeting for yuletide.

The best Christmas party I could think of is a yule log on the fire, a house smelling of spicy green branches, a table lit by scarlet candles, a hot savory dinner; and for guests, the homefolks, and a few dearly loved friends. A bowl of punch with a circle of blue and green and yellow and bronze pottery cups around it. And after dinner someone reads aloud Dickens' *Christmas Carol*. The firelight flickers, the punch sparkles in the cups, the children eat hot, buttery popcorn. "God bless us every one," cried Tiny Tim.

I wish everyone could have such a Christmas, with peace on earth a reality. I wish we could all say on Christmas night:

"God rest you merry, gentlemen,
Let nothing you dismay."

January

Song for January

What time I wandered where the dogwood
  grows
I felt white blossoms falling on my breast,
Forgetting easily how fall the snows
Upon the stripped tree winter has
  possessed.
Today I walk beneath this sterile sky,
Finding it difficult to fix my mind
On greening branches proudly lifting high
A silver freight unscarred by winter wind.

So short a season has the memory,
So apt a pupil, lessoned by the frost,
While yet the undefeated dogwood tree
Shelters the sap, nor counts the season lost.

Wherefore, my heart, be not so poor a
  thing,
Believe in this, the dogwood blooms next
  spring!

WHEN I WAS a child, no one had ever heard of organized winter sports. Ski trains and snow trains were undreamed of. The trains that ran through our little town carried people who were going to Milwaukee to shop, or even as far as Chicago, on business; but traveling was a serious thing, not to be undertaken lightly. It involved so much packing and unpacking, and tucking washcloths in rubber bags, and nightgowns in silk envelope affairs. But now people leap on trains with a small slide-fastened bag, and go anywhere. Girls tie their hair up in a scarf, put on slacks, and sit happily waxing skis as the train slides over the winter countryside.

However, we did enjoy winter. There was a horse named Grace who alternately acted as what we called "the hearse horse" and as a puller of a long, homemade bobsled. The sled belonged to a boy named Eugene, and as soon as snow began to pile up along the fences everyone began to do favors for Eugene. It was a little odd, but I never "got mad with" Eugene in sleighing time. In midsummer I might become involved in those strange adolescent sufferings, but not in January. We would bundle up in galoshes and Mackinaws and woollen hoods and fur mittens and pile on the bobsled and Grace would move slowly down the snowy streets, earning her twenty-five cents an hour the easy way.

The air was always like a clean, quick knife blade, and the sun frozen gold, and the shadows of the snow ruts fell blue behind us. We sang "Long, Long Trail," and I was almost in tune, but not quite. The boys fell off and scuffled in the snow and threw snowballs, and if a boy was really wild about you, he showed his ardor by putting snow down your neck. And at the end of the afternoon we went home for oyster stew and hot buttered crackers, cocoa and cake.

Oyster stew was really oyster stew then. Mother made it by melting half a cup of butter in a big, heavy pan. She added a quart of oysters and let them just come to a boil, then poured over them three cups of milk and a cup of cream, a teaspoon of salt, a half teaspoon of pepper. This simmered until the oysters began to rise to the top; then it was served with parsley, paprika, and often more butter on top.

We used to have winter picnics, too. This involved a long ride on a streetcar, a hike through the woods, carrying all our supplies, and a struggle to get the door open to a summer cottage by the lake. The parents thought we were demented and expected us to get pneumonia, but perseverance usually won out and we could go, if we came home before dark. Nothing in the world, I am sure, is so cold as a summer cottage in January. It is far colder than outdoors, colder than an Alpine hut. Building the fire was a mammoth task. The fireplace smoked from the cold, the wood was covered with snow that melted and ran into the small flame. But in the end, after much harder work than our parents ever got from us, we had a fire. A lovely big blazing fire. Then we unpacked the lunch and thawed it out, and cooked smoky hamburgers and frankfurters and boiled coffee madly with eggshells.

We sat around the fire, still wrapped in sixteen layers of clothing, and ate, and talked the queer talk of youth. Outside, the lake stretched its miles of frozen gray-green. The shores of Fond-du-lac were bleak and cold against the horizon. The line of closed summer cottages was dark and still and the sound of our voices echoed along empty verandas.

"What did you ever find to do, when you were growing up?" the children ask, as they dash from movie to movie, dance to dance.

"Oh, we used to go on winter picnics," we say.

"But what for?"

Here is a strange thing. In summer I always make plans for those long winter nights. I say blithely, "Well, in the long winter evenings I am really going to learn to knit socks. There will be time, then, to reread all of Shakespeare and the Elizabethan poets." On a long winter evening we can refile the phonograph records, straighten the game cupboard, and really throw out those incomplete checker sets and nibbled game boards. A thousand small, niggling jobs we can dash off, I think, in winter.

Every single year I go through this happy reasoning and every year, in surprise, I face the fact in January, that those long winter evenings are pure fiction. Possibly the pioneers had them, but I doubt it. I imagine that after a rugged bout with cooking and weaving and scrubbing, my pioneer housekeeper simply heated the soapstone for her rope bed and climbed in and pulled the feather bed around her ears and went to sleep!

Sometimes my city friends ask me, with sympathy, if the long winter evenings aren't dreary. No theater, no concert, no ballet. What do we do with ourselves?

What does become of those evenings? I often wonder. Because I find myself, in January, saying cheerfully, and with hope, "Now when the summer evenings come, and it stays light so long, I can really catch up with those odd jobs. I'll just wait for summer."

I suspect it is just a human weakness to look forward to a season with plenty of leisure, a tranquil space between regular jobs. Much the way we used to anticipate nice restful vacations. And then actually we wore ourselves out on those nice restful vacations.

I wish we had kept the Indian way of calling a time a Moon of Hunting, a Moon of Corn — if there was a moon of corn. I call January the Moon of Stoves. This is the time when it is pleasant to gather in the big kitchen around the old black range and lift out the bean pot from the comfortable oven.

We have a fine electric stove in the middle kitchen, and it has its own elegant, streamlined personality. It is a modern invention, better than emeralds to own. Turning a switch and getting the immaculate, hot cooking power is a fine thing. I say my best for it.

But also give me an old-fashioned range. House is not home without one. The kitchen is as warm as new-buttered toast. The chunky stove wood sends a good smell out when you lift the lid, almost like burning leaves on an autumn hill. The soup pot simmers gently in the back corner. We eat at the table right near the stove, and bask in its warmth.

I like the way you can get any gradation of heat by just pushing your pan an inch to the right or an inch to the left. And the way the oven cooks so slowly, the rich meat juices just seal themselves in the roast.

We have two kitchens, and we call one the back kitchen, and one the middle kitchen. This often confuses guests. I shout from upstairs, "You'll find it in the middle kitchen!" and if they are not used to our peculiar, unlogical family vocabulary, they may be found later in the taproom, and nobody knows why that room is called the taproom, either!

But the back kitchen belongs especially to the Moon of Stoves. The popcorn in the evening! The stuffed spareribs on a blizzardy noon! Honey by the oven, lifting a golden nose to smell what Mamma has inside the stove this time. Esmé climbing happily into the oven when the fire dies down. I am sure few people keep cats in the oven, but Stillmeadow has them there. It is highly unsanitary, and only people who also belong to Siamese cats could possibly understand this.

Melody, the darling puppy, pokes a black satin head from under the range. And that's another thing! In the middle kitchen there is no waste space under the electric stove. It has drawers and warming ovens and tray racks. But there is no waste space under the range either, really. It is always packed solidly with cockers. They feel, in January, that a stove equipped with a full quota of spaniels really completes the furnishing.

We had a fancy heater in the back kitchen until it rusted out. Every time we lighted a fire, smoke poured from a thousand places. So we retired it. Bob and Jill and I sallied to Waterbury to find a range.

It was a typical family excursion. I got lost, we almost got arrested, and we came home with not only a stove but a crate of green grapes.

We went from store to store and, Waterbury having been laid out by some Indian who was undoubtedly under the influence of firewater, we never found a street that went where we wanted to go. Bob would drive madly around the block, using up our rationed gas in a horrible way, while Jill and I dived from basement to basement. All dealers keep their stoves in the basement.

Finally I ran ahead, leaving Jill to

inspect one place and Bob to park. I had a large flashlight because George, the mainstay of our kennel, told me earnestly that I must look inside at the firebrick. As I loped down the crowded street, intent on the chase, I wondered why everybody seemed to fall back in surprise and then turn and look after me. Heads were craned from stores. Drivers leaned from passing cars.

"I must have aged terribly in three days," I thought sadly. "Or maybe it's this red shirt that used to be Don's. Maybe they don't feel middle-aged women should wear red shirts." After about six blocks, the truth came to me. There I was, dashing down a blazing hot street, in dazzling sunshine, holding a mammoth flashlight in my lifted right hand. I had too much else in my arms to hide it, but I did turn it backward.

We found the range. Bob parked the car.

A policeman materialized instantly. "It's going to cost you six dollars to park here," he said happily, getting out his pad.

I was buying an antique flatiron at the moment, and a loaf of Italian bread from the next shop, and I saw him.

"Run, Jill, run!" I screamed, "Bob's arrested!"

She ran, carrying a length of stovepipe in her arms. The secondhand man ran after her with the legs of the stove, muttering that his heart wasn't so good any more.

The policeman gave in. And when he saw the pieces of our range lying on the walk, he said warmly, "Stay as long as you need to," and went on.

So the stove came home. I had a feeling that it was happy to be set up in a home again, polished and come to life. I wondered what other home it had lived in, how many little children had warmed their hands by it. George came over and set it up, Jill got out the stove polish, and I couldn't wait to stir up onions and peppers and olive oil and get them simmering on it.

It is only now and then that people really speak to each other from the curious secret depths in us all. I wonder whether it is Anglo-Saxon reticence, or just a human inability to communicate. Or a fear of being thought queer. However it may be, there is a wall around most people most of the time. We all go on living on the surface like water bugs, and most of our lives seem just about as aimless as their courses. Now and then, in a crisis, we cry from the secret place, "Oh, be close to me!" Perhaps the loneliness is eased a moment, but the next time the loved one says brightly, "What are you thinking about?" you will answer, "Oh, just about making a devil's food cake."

I remember once meeting my most adored uncle after a long absence. My heart was full of things I wished to discuss with him; I needed his wisdom, his steadiness. He was, of all men, the one who "saw life steadily and saw it whole." He also wished to communicate with me. We sat together a long time.

"What did you talk about?" I was asked afterward.

"Oh, we just sat there not telling each other things," I answered.

And yet, really, we did communicate after all. "You are getting to look like your mother," he said. Then he took off his glasses and polished them on his immaculate handkerchief. "There seems to be a mist on my glasses," he said. A mist on his glasses! I never saw him again. But I have a dear memory of that moment that I shall always keep.

As Christmas and the New Year come and go again, I feel as if I should like to break down the walls, and to urge everyone else to break them down, and actually speak from the heart to one another. I wish I could gather all the people who are dear to me in front of the fire, not in a mass, but one at a time, and give them my own holiday message.

Like this: "I want to tell you that all my life you have been an inspiration to me. You have borne heavy burdens with gaiety and good will, you have accepted loss with humor and fortitude. And you have cared about the small successes of your friends. There is, my dear friend, a glowing warmth in your spirit."

And like this: "I want you to know on this New Year's Eve how much I admire and love you. I love you for your clear swift thinking, your indomitable will, your vitality in a rather tired world, your keen, creative spirit. It is impossible to be intimate with you because of the impersonality which is part of you;

nevertheless, I respect your integrity."

And this: "I know you are thinking of me as just another finger wave, as you go about your long day of hairdressing. But I am not just a customer, because I appreciate your personality. I have gleaned a good deal of information about you, while I sat under the drier, or had the ends turned up. You have worked hard; you have had a difficult life; your family situation is almost unbearable; you haven't much money, and the future is not going to bring you any great gifts. But you have a homely philosophy that carries you along without any complaining. You are both sensible and cheerful. You are a great person. I know a number of wealthy and intellectual and important people who could well be humble in your presence."

Of course, I shall never say these things. I shall say, instead, "Let me give you another cup of coffee." And, "Have you read the new serial in the Post?" And, "Yes, I guess I will have a rinse today."

It would be rather nice, though, to make the holidays a time of gifts, not wrapped in tissue paper, but gifts of the heart.

My respect for the people of the South-west has mounted to awe. A friend in Albuquerque sent me a present of a package of Mexican beans and a box of real chili. The chili sauce is easy to make, like a white sauce. You are supposed to add as much water as you like to make the sauce thick or thin, and then stir in smoothly two tablespoons of chili powder.

I made it last week-end. The beans smelled delicious, tender and golden brown in the pot. I dished out huge platefuls — we all like beans — and then ladled the sauce over. I took a generous mouthful and almost rose to the ceiling. I felt as if I had swallowed a furnace fire. For five minutes I couldn't even speak, and that is a rare thing with me.

My friend wrote, "If you don't like it so hot, you can use less chili." And from now on, I shall certainly use less chili. About a teaspoon, I think. Maybe I can work up gradually to the New Mexican ideal; I hate to be strangled by a delicacy.

Bonnie's puppies are five weeks old. Bonnie wasn't supposed to have them — it was a love match. Windy is the father, and thinks nothing of it. Bonnie is black and white, but there are four solid black babies, and one little Windy, a miniature copy in paler red. The color variations in cockers make puppies an endless wonder. I should think it would surprise Bonnie herself, whose last litter was all parti-color. Since I have to be in the city during school and work months, a good neighbor and dog raiser took Bonnie in. Now his kitchen is full of tumbling balls of fur, and Bonnie considers herself a queen in her own kingdom. Little Windy has the same look as his father, innocent and naïve; he has the short, sturdy body, and good straight front, and a wagging morsel of tail.

The black sisters are pert and bouncy, and have already decided to spend their lives in people's laps. They keep climbing out of the basket and falling plump on the floor, and making staggering little rushes to get to the nearest person. Bonnie has the idea they may be a nuisance; she doesn't think having a family is much fun anymore. Now the lady who takes care of them is feeding them three-hour extra snacks, giving them sun baths on a card table, and generally introducing them to the world.

There is always one puppy who doesn't want to drink milk and has to be persuaded. Usually a male. And one who intends to wade in the milk, whether or no. Then there is the fighter, who grabs brother's ears and swings on them; who pounces. A pounce consists of collecting all four paws, no mean feat in itself, and then wavering through the air and falling heavily on the victim, and in three seconds going heavily to sleep, stomach up, paws limp.

We wean the puppies on undiluted evaporated milk. This is richer than raw milk and never varies. They get scraped raw beef as soon as their teeth prick through, beginning with a thumbnail apiece. Egg yolks and dry cereal come next, and tomato juice and cod liver oil. The two main rules are that the food be warm, and that everything be cut in very small pieces. This is true for the whole life of spaniels. They never do well with hunks of food. We use all kinds of prepared baby foods for the puppies, and find them wonderful. If a puppy has a good start he will be a healthy dog all his life, barring accident.

Star and Pussy are beginning to look like small black Teddy bears again. I wonder if all blacks get heavier coats in winter than the other spaniel colors. Windy gets redder and Saxon shines more lustrously. They all had baths before the holidays. We got the back kitchen stove red-hot and warmed the towels on the rack. After a good scrubbing each dog is moved to a grooming table and rubbed dry. Then they all tear around the warm room for a bit, following which they are brushed with a stiff brush. I think the fact that we almost never have any skin difficulty in the kennel is due partly to the diet and partly to the fact that we keep the dogs' skins clean and free from parasites. But in winter we are careful about having them warm and dry.

They all seem to have crystal-gazing balls when we are contemplating shampoos. We may sneak around surreptitiously with towels and spell out b-a-t-h in a whisper. It's no good. The first thing we know there isn't a spaniel in sight. The place is dogless. Even the ingenuous Windy feels something in the air and scuttles into Bob's room, under the bed. Sister always hides behind the kitchen door, made small into a black and white ball. Honey gets under the middle of my bed, her favorite retreat in trouble.

One by one, reluctant cockers are pulled out by members of the family standing on their heads, crawling on hands and knees. After the cockers are all clean and dry and shining, the washers need baths themselves. Then a snack is indicated.

Last week-end we had guests from a long way off, from Colombia and Guatemala. And a guest from a homestead family in Wyoming. The countries have been chiefly colored spots on the map to me before, or part of an abstract thing called International Relationships. And Wyoming has just been a state I have never seen, but which has to do with the old wild West.

Sitting in front of the apple wood fire in this little New England house, we ate rosy, home-grown Baldwin apples and toasted cheese sandwiches, and comfortable talk filled the room, while two cockers tried to sit on Carlos' lap, and a black cat perched on Luis' shoulder. Bettina was curled up on the sofa with Cicely, hunting up the best Latin-American records to play.

Cicely put on "Noche de Ronda," and brought in another bowl of apples. The men began to talk of home, and suddenly Colombia and Guatemala were no longer colored sections on a map; they were the places where our friends lived. The houses, the families, the way of life began to seem real. I imagined the servant going every morning to the market, everything fresh every day, because refrigeration is so rare. And everything growing all the season round, so canning and preserving are unnecessary. So Carlos had to see the freezer, with six months' supplies packed in it — broccoli, corn, spinach, chicken, raspberries, strawberries, mince pies. Then the ironer and the washing machine and the electric range and the heaters fascinated him. Of course, in his home a family of two has five servants. But, he said, each servant does only one thing.

One markets, one cooks, one makes beds.

"I like this way better," he said. "Here you have everything in equipment, everything so clean and efficient. When you have many servants you have many difficulties also."

I looked at the washing machine with new respect. It never quarrels or talks back or argues about how much work it does. Maybe I wouldn't be much happier with five servants at four dollars apiece a month, after all. The more we talked the more I appreciated the things we have to work with.

Later on Luis, a doctor, got out pictures of his wife, and two grave-eyed, lovely babies. He had left them for a long time in order to study in the United States and carry his knowledge to his country. His wife had a lovely, delicate beauty; intelligent dark eyes and a wistful mouth. And suddenly I thought about this little family and their contribution to the world, and I wondered how many North Americans the doctor would meet who would respect this.

When we had dinner, the two men wiped the dishes for the girls, and half the time Spanish, half the time English sounded over the rattle of the silver. And the laughter was in the same universal language. Then in the morning Carlos said proudly, "I do up my bed."

I wondered how many North Americans would adjust so easily and gaily to a different way, for simple housework must have been very strange and new to them.

After breakfast the two girls and Carlos went for a walk, so Bettina could see the trees. How wonderful were the trees, she said. She had never seen a tree close at hand except the Chinese elm at home. The great, latticed branches of the old quiet trees were a mystery and a wonder to her. They are a mystery and a wonder to me, too, and yet they are so familiar one easily takes them for granted.

The doctor said shyly, "May I play the phonograph, please?"

I nodded and went on peeling potatoes for dinner. Then I laid down the knife and listened in amazement. He was not playing "Borrachita," or "La Comparsita." He was playing, "I am the Lord High Executioner," from *The Mikado*. I went into the front room and he was beaming over the phonograph, radiant. Gilbert and Sullivan he had heard as a child in Guatemala and he loved them. I did not need any lectures on world brotherhood; it was right in my own farmhouse.

"The world," I thought, "is just full of folks, and all those far, strange places I may never see, are really the homes of my friends. For we are all kin, no matter what tongue we speak, and just as soon as everyone realizes it, what a world we shall have!"

My father sang those songs to me, when I was a child in Wisconsin, and the doctor from Guatemala heard them as a child in Latin America, and now we hummed the gay tunes together. "A wandering minstrel I, a thing of shreds and patches —" "He polished up the handle so carefully, that now he is the ruler of the Queen's Navee."

"Thank you very, very much," he said, as he turned the last record.

And with a burst of pride, I summoned up my best, "De nada," I said, "It's nothing."

Actually, though, if we speak the same

language with our hearts, the language we speak with our lips is not so important.

Now when we walk down the snowy road, we often cut some evergreen branches for the house. A beautiful arrangement can be made in an old white ironstone tureen — mixed evergreens and three scarlet geraniums from the window box. I make mine with the branches for the height, and a focal point of the geraniums in a triangle near the base of the container. It is dramatic and beautiful, and lasts a long time.

Begonia cuttings make nice bouquets, too, and if you leave them in water long enough, they usually root, and there you have a new set for another window box or row of pots. The begonia is an amazing plant, anyway; it just keeps going along and blooming, and when cut back, it starts up again.

The summer flowers are a memory now, but the house still looks loved with the green arrangements in ironstone or shining copper bowl.

It is a good thing to curl up with a book for a little while before bedtime. I like

James Russell Lowell, saying, "Solitude is as needful to the imagination as society is wholesome for the character." We all need to spend some time alone; people who cannot bear their own company for a time have thin souls.

The deep part of winter gives most of us a little more time alone. The natural rhythm of time has changed from that of summer. But instead of dreading the dark winter days, we ought to savor them for what they can give. Now there should be time to reread old books, to absorb some philosophy, to play a whole symphony without hurrying. Meanwhile, I dip into Keats, or read a little of the magic of the Irish poets.

"I hear the shadowy horses, their
    long manes a-shake,
  Their hoofs heavy with tumult,
    their eyes glimmering white;
  The north unfolds above the
    clinging, creeping night —"

Yesterday I struggled through the deep snow to the brook, with Honey floundering after me. She went like a seal in surf, a golden seal in a white surf. Down in the hollow the tall dead weeds are still standing, the color of old bronze and saffron, and beaver brown. There were the delicate prints of a rabbit and the wild, light touch of a fox in the still snow. How strange the silence sounds when the birds have gone to far places! And yet, to a careful ear, there are special sounds that are lovely. The sound of running water under the ice sheath of the brook is one, and Honey and I stopped to listen to it. It has a magic all its own, the sound of living water. Where the ice is nothing but lace, I can look down and see the black brook water thrusting its course over the cold rock.

And this is a wonderful thing, at the end of an old year, at the beginning of a new year, to see how the brook flows on. I tell Honey about it, and she lifts her dark amber eyes and looks at me steadily. There is enough beauty in this world, I tell her, for every man to brim his heart with. And all we have to do is put away the hard things of life awhile and look at our world all over again.

It takes an open mind and a ready heart to appreciate winter in New England.

The wind blows, the snow piles deep, the car gets stuck, and pipes freeze. It is easy to dream of the South Sea Islands, with coral beaches and sapphire water and strange fruits dropping in your hand. And beautiful natives with garlands of frangipani playing dreamy music on odd instruments. I always think of frangipani as a cross between a camellia and a chrysanthemum.

But under the hard and bitter rind of winter, there is much loveliness. The white mystery of snow is a splendid thing, all the landscape is muted to deep silver laced with blue shadows. The meadow is a sea of pearl with scattered dark masts of briar riding the foam. The apple orchards pattern the sky with drypoint precision. The cool clean smell of snow is in the air, a special fragrance known only to winter country.

The sounds are fine, too. The ring of skates on black ice, the laughter of children making snowmen, and the soft thud of hooves as the horses stamp in the barn on a frosty morning. The crackle of applewood in the fireplace. The feathery sound of snow shifting from the pine branches in the woods. And the small busy sounds of popcorn bursting in the pan.

Yes, there is much to be said for winter. If one looks directly for its beauty.

Beginning the New Year is a good time to renew one's faith. To resolve again to live just a little larger life. I like the lines — I think they are Katherine Lee Bates':

"That which thou wilt be, thou art.
  As the oak, astir in the acorn
  The dull earth rendeth apart,
  So thou, the seed of they longing,
  Breaketh and waketh the heart."

These are lines to savor, to say over again in the mind. No night is so dark as to lack a star, even a January night. That reminds me of more favorite lines:

"My night shall be remembered for
  a star,
  That outshone all the suns of all
  men's days."

We don't have much to say about what the new year will bring. We have learned to go on the best we can, and be thankful for whatever we have. Nothing, I thought, looking around the firelit circle, can take away from anyone on earth the love of his or her dear ones. You can't blow up love with a bomb, or shoot it down with a machine gun. Courage remains stronger than fire or sword. Loyalty lies too deep for depth charges to shatter it. And real patriotism is as bright now as it was in that terrible winter at Valley Forge, when that stubborn fellow, General George Washington, brought an army through on faith. The real things go on.

February

Song for February

They race across the snow with flying feet,
The red, the black, the black-and-white,
   and gold,
Spaniels at play, light as blown leaves, and
   fleet,
Winging their ears, and sniffing the still
   cold.
The good far scent of fox is in the air,
And rabbit print assails the velvet nose,
Secret the silver weasel keeps his lair,
Swift slides the mink along the reedy close.

Eyes that are eager, hearts that beat so
   loud,
Oh wild and lovely freedom they possess,
The Spaniel hunters, they the brave and
   proud,
Dreaming their dream of conquered
   wilderness.

How vast a kingdom then is mine, who see
How swift they turn and leave the hunt for
   me!

THE NEW ENGLAND countryside is now deep in winter. The wind blows wild and dark up the hill and batters the house. The great maples lose any branches that are dying; they crash down in the night and start the cockers barking like mad. Some days the snow drifts over the fencetops, and then the wind comes again and bare ground shows.

Our forefathers were sturdy men and wise to weather; they knew how to build for this winter wind. The house is low toward the north, the roof slants steeply. The barns faced the wind, too, and the cattle sheltered in the lee of the building.

All down the valley the little white houses are snugged down in February, and many of them have close-packed branches of evergreen banked around the foundation.

I like to go across to the neighbor's barn at dusk and stand inside where the cows are being milked. The air is steamy and warm from the heat of the cows, and smells of fresh milk and sweet hay. As George milks, the sound of the milk falling into the clean pail is a pleasant sound. There are always waiting kittens, and the big dog wags his way into the warmth. The kittens get a dish of warm milk, and their little tongues lap so delicately as they drink.

The cows stand quietly, turning their heads to look at me with mild surprise. I always wonder what cows think about. They seem content, but perhaps they, too, have yearnings for a life of ranging the woods, free and leading their own lives.

One of my favorite legends is the story of Europa and the beautiful milk-white bull, who was Zeus in disguise and who bore the beautiful maiden away over the blue sea. It is a story filled with enchantment, with the singing light of the gold sun, the meadow sprinkled with blue and white flowers, the sea sparkling on a dreamy shore and the young girl with her arms filled with the blossoms. No wonder the god loved her. The white bull was suddenly beside her and she probably dropped the flowers, half afraid and half wondering — I'm sure his hoofs and horns were silver — and then she wreathed the horns in garlands of blue and gold, and rode away to immortality. The world was innocent and young when the gods came down and dwelt with mortals whenever they were bored with Olympus!

We need to keep the old legends alive in our matter-of-fact world. This month has its own legend, the tale of St. Valentine. I hope we always celebrate Valentine's Day. The making of valentines was a serious business when I was growing up. Gilt and silver paper, red hearts, lacy paper frills, blue ribbons, and little doves to paste on the finished product — we loved them all. I usually got my doves on upside down, but I thought they were elegant. Does anyone ever forget the excitement of that large valentine signed in masculine scrawl GUESS WHO?

It had its hazards too. There was always a girl who got more valentines than anyone else. And a boy who got only a few funny ones. My mother had them in mind when she arranged for us to have extras. It was possible to increase some girl's quota in a hurry, or add a few for the boy.

Later on, when we were older, there was Valentine's Day when the only boy in the world produced a package from his pocket with a present in it. Really better than Christmas, for everyone exchanged gifts for Christmas, but a real Valentine, not just candy — that was something. Oh, enchanted winter moon shining down on two bent heads, on mittened hands! The paper crackled, the ribbon was folded away, and there it was, the little locket set with chips of what might be diamonds, or the silver ring with the matrix stone. Who ever forgets first love, and the first real valentine?

It's catalogue time again, and there's never so fair a garden as the one that grows during a blizzard — on the colorful pages of the seed books. The seedsmen ought to be subsidized by the government, because their catalogues bring hope of spring and summer to winter-worn folk. In the postman's bag lie orchards and rose gardens, and acres of bouncing vegetables, all done in brown paper. And it seems a miracle to me that for a few cents you can buy beauty and nourishment, and I wonder what the seedsmen buy that's half as precious as the stuff they sell!

"Now this year we mustn't put in anything new," said Bob.

But that was in August. And Jill, the gardener, agreed firmly, "No, there's no room for anything more."

That was all right in August, but in winter it never looks as though we had anything at all in the yard except two rather doubtful holly bushes, and a couple of little switches with cages around them which Jill believes are Seckel pears. Quite often we have planted new things eagerly in the spring right on top of what we set out late in the fall before. In many ways our garden is a survival of the fittest. We don't seem to be suited to the making of garden plans; not even Jill, the methodical one. She is always writing down in notebooks and I am always losing them, so if we had a garden plan we couldn't find it.

Last night the snow fell heavy and soft. Jill and Bob were making out orders, while I ranged dreamily through weedless, bugless, unblighted and unspanieled gardens. Jill sat at the desk, business-like, writing down figures.

Bob, from the depths of the wing chair, said hopefully, "I'm going to try lupines again. You know, it said to scratch the seeds. Sometimes I wonder if I scratched them too much. Funny they never came up at all. And I'm going to try ruffled sweet peas."

"Souvenir de Claudius Pernet," I murmured.

"Onions," said Jill.

"Chinese delphinium," said Bob.

"Carrots," said Jill.

"Golden Sunset climbers," I decided. Such a pretty picture.

"Beets," said Jill.

"Jill, look at the copper climbers," I urged.

Jill laid down her pencil. "You and Bob spend all your time on flowers," she said, "but when it's time to eat, I notice my vegetables are pretty important."

I said, "All I want is this nice lily collection."

"Lilies!" Bob looked up. "For heaven's sake, lilies! I had to chop a path with an axe through those old day lilies last year when I wanted to take a picture of

Cicely by my dogwood tree."

"That's just it," I was triumphant, "they'll grow. They like stones and things. I shall plant something that doesn't have to be fed with a teaspoon." I am notoriously poor as a wielder of fertilizer. Most of it smells bad.

"The lily pictures are awfully pretty, too," I said. I always buy by the picture. Nothing ever comes up and looks like any picture in any book, but I still pick out the most attractive cuts.

At last we met on common ground over the gladiolus. We are all gladiolus fiends — and I use the word fiends advisedly. Glads possess you, if you like them. The colors are so lovely they ache in me, and the flowers are so proud and vibrant on the clean blade of the stalk. My favorites are the soft coppery shades, the dim lavenders, the luminous golds, and the pure translucent whites. This year we added Duna, Wasaga, Heavenly Blue, Mother Machree, and Bagdad to our color symphony. Pelegrina is an old favorite in the blue-purple variety. Golden Dream and Gate of Heaven, in the yellows, are excellent, and almost worth buying for their names. I do wish all flowers could be called by imaginative names. Who wouldn't rather grow a Golden Dream than an Al Smith? Al Smith is pink. My favorite pink is Picardy. Evensong and Marmora and Mother Machree I like for the smoky shades. Bagdad is even more gorgeous.

The black-red makes me think of Joseph Conrad, someway, and I decide to read *The Nigger of the Narcissus* and *The Arrow of Gold* again. The white is like the best of Tennyson's lyrics.

We finally got our orders ready. Mine was a little odd, perhaps: roses and lilies and a weeping willow. Bob, steadfast and undefeated after several failures, listed lupines, double hollyhocks, a butterfly bush, and two blue gardenia campanulas. Jill firmly ordered a dozen Alfred blackberry bushes and almost weakened over more peach trees. She dotes on peach trees. Then came the vegetables, and already in fancy I am getting out the pressure cooker to can!

I was reminded of this scene years later, when we were first urged to make victory gardens. I sighed and said, "I'm sorry for the people who are just starting. Think of all they have to learn."

"Nonsense," said Jill briskly. "All you do is plant the seeds. That's how we began."

I looked at her in amazement. "For three years solid," I said, "you did nothing but study that garden. Garden books. Government bulletins. Encyclopedias. Every minute you weren't out hoeing and weeding you were reading about it."

When I pointed this out Jill said, "Maybe we did have to learn a little."

My heart goes out to beginners. The first year, while wheeling in squash by the wheelbarrow loads, we had exactly five and a half strawberries. Now, after all the years they have been at it, Bob and Jill are both in the expert class. They know how many carrots grow from a package, and even I have learned that the size of a seed has little to do with what comes of it. And looking back over it on this wintry day, I realize that probably few things are so rewarding as gardens, no matter how many mistakes you make learning.

One of my friends suggested that I devote part of the new year to studying birds. So I made a resolution to that effect, although I already seem to have more interests than one lifetime will adequately supply time for. Actually, I can't think of a better thing to do than begin a new interest for the new year.

Jill said, "What with photography and vegetables and dogs and children and literature and cooking and fishing and flowers and music, we have almost enough interests, I should think. Not to mention making furniture and working jigsaw puzzles."

"I don't make furniture," I pointed out. "I can't saw straight. You make the furniture."

"Yes, but if you take up birds, I know who will have to get up at five and gallop around looking them up," she finished. "It'll be me. When you canned all those mixed vegetables, I noticed that I scraped quite a horde of potatoes and things."

Her canny reference to early morning did bother me. I never could see why bird fanciers have to get up at daybreak and lope around over a damp landscape to commune with the birds. Birds, I think, ought to hang around at reasonable hours. Maybe I wouldn't get very excited identifying a blue-billed whatnot, when I hadn't had a good, hot breakfast. On the other hand, there is this whole world of nature, this various and complete life, that I am stranger to; and that is a sad thought.

Jill got me an impressive bird book to begin with. After studying it hard, I was greatly troubled.

"How can you tell all these things," I asked, "unless the birds come up and sit on your lap?"

"You get field glasses," said Jill.

I felt even more doubtful. I never have been adept at focusing opera glasses. Just as I get the right end to my eye, and screw the things up, whatever I am viewing moves away and I only see odd blurs and table legs. I should never catch anything so flighty as a bird.

I went into one of my customary reveries, trying to go back to any birds I had known. There were the canaries, three of them, and they fought so the whole house was full of feathers and sand from the cage. We had to keep them in separate cages, and then they sulked in silence. The canary interval was a lurid one. When they weren't sulking, they amused themselves tearing up newspapers and strewing them from the cages. They had a kind of feverish intensity which you wouldn't expect in a canary. They did everything but sing.

Then I remembered the parrot I met in Charlottesville, Virginia. As I entered the elegant library with a friend, politely gloved and hatted and ready to be formally introduced, this parrot stuck her head out of her cage, lifted one claw carelessly and then burst into a wild shriek of laughter. Considerably embarrassed, I smoothed my skirt and gave myself a hasty glance in the mirror over the mantel. The hostess advanced, and I put out a tentative hand. The parrot threw back her head and yelled with mirth. Nobody could doubt that she thought I was the funniest sight any bird ever saw.

I said, "Hello, Polly."

"Ha-ha-ha."

My formal call was over as soon as I could manage. As I left the house, I involuntarily looked back. There was the parrot in the window, one eye gleaming at me, and as she saw me go, she almost fell off her perch with hysterics. I was so shaken I found I had lost my gloves.

But I have one memory that is not funny. I was so full of sorrow on this particular day that I did not see how I could keep going. It was February then, too, and the day was as cold and dark as my own grief. Snow drifted high over the fences, and the sky was grey and dim. I went out, because the house shut my grief in so close, and I drove out from the little town to the country, where there was no sign of life or movement anywhere. And then suddenly I came over the edge of a snowy hill, and there on a broken fence rail, sat a cardinal, scarlet in the snow. He was swaying back and forth, and his light, alive body caught all the light there was.

I stopped and looked, and he cocked his head at me and then flew up into the greyness with a flash of scarlet wings. All at once I was comforted, hope and strength were renewed in my heart like a miracle. Just because a redbird perched on a winter fence rail.

Thinking about birds, I decided to go and look at Mr. Smith's white pigeons. Don went with me, and we drove in the fresh, cold morning along the winding road toward Roxbury. The cats and bunnies deflected us slightly, but we walked on with Mr. Smith to the edge of the pine woods where the long, low buildings lay. We climbed the wooden steps and entered a place of pigeons.

Beautiful in the dusky light were the white birds, hundreds of white wings moved softly, and the sweet melancholy sound of cooing murmured in the air. Their delicate little feet were garnet-colored, and their eyes were like fire opals. They weren't even afraid of us; they stepped around proudly, arching their necks and making their soft sound.

The new babies were in a room of their own with pleasant warm nests. "They haven't any hair at all," said Don, in amazement. They were all legs and necks and about the color of new-baked bread. It was true they had no feathers.

All the way home Don and I discussed the possibility of white pigeons. But we can't have pigeons for a little while, we decided. It's the same old problem: we can raise only things that can increase indefinitely and happily, without having to be eaten, or sold to be eaten. This narrows the field frightfully, although Jill says we shall have hens yet, and a nice, calm Jersey cow.

The problem of Christmas dinner was serious last year. Miss Nellie, the lady who helps us keep house, had raised five very noble geese, with the idea that one should be served forth for our Christmas dinner. She raised them at her house, and they turned out to be house pets, following her everywhere, waddling placidly in her wake like a small, solemn flotilla. All summer she kept telling me of the cute things the geese did, until finally I said firmly, "We can't eat those geese. We can't do it."

I refused, myself, to get acquainted with them, knowing my own weakness full well. I couldn't eat a sirloin if I had ever spoken to the cow that — well, anyway, I was worried.

As November wore on, I noticed that she, herself, grew reluctant. Nothing saved her except the fact that she was brought up on a Vermont farm and has a good deal of the stoic in her. At the last hour she induced a neighbor to come and kill one. Then Miss Nellie and her niece spent three hours plucking it.

The goose appeared the next morning, impersonally resting in a roaster. I paid very little attention to it, but when the savory odor of roasting goose began to fill the air, I felt marvelously restored. And when the family gathered around the table and the goose came in, such a sigh of delight rose that I decided the poor goose had died in a noble cause.

February is not a good month for cooks. One gets tired of winter food and it is too early for spring dishes. But a friend sent me a recipe for Cranberry Island stew which really gave us a lift.

Two pounds of beef stew with the marrow bone included, cooked slowly until the beef begins to get tender, are the beginning. Mrs. Murphy says she adds a few sprigs of her own summer savory, a sliced onion, and salt and pepper. About an hour before dinner she adds three or four small beets, raw, peeled and cut into quarters. After another fifteen minutes she adds a peeled, sliced turnip, and when the beets and turnip are almost tender, three or more carrots, cut into fingers, and four small potatoes, peeled and cut into halves. Cook slowly until vegetables are done, having enough liquid for plenty of gravy. Serve in soup plates with the delicious gravy. This may also be made with the bones and bits of meat from a roast. Lamb or veal may be used if you have no beef.

Now that our New England is like a refrigerator that somebody went away and left too long, I often wish I could turn the month to defrost — just long enough, please, for a breathing spell between sleet and sleet. A defrosted fifth of February, for instance, and then wash the whole landscape with soda and warm water and start over again. Instead, the wind is beating a hollow drum and the sleet hissing against the storm windows. I am always surprised to realize that sleet does actually hiss, because hissing should be a hot sound.

Esmé and Tigger sit right smack on the radiators, and when we pick them up, their fur is like hot embers. Esmé has a remote and dreamy blue gaze; part of her spirit has gone away to a tropic land where a pink-luster moon shines and little silver fish play in the warm shallows of a blue lagoon. Very few things give one such a sense of comfort as a cat on a hot radiator or in the ashes at the edge of the fireplace, though I hardly know why it should be so. I feel fortified against February just by looking at her.

Melody and Hildegarde skip over the crusty snow like winter butterflies, Melody blacker than satin, and Hildegarde marked snow on velvet. Something gay and wild comes to their hearts with the winter weather; I believe their mother told them legends about the land of everlasting ice and snow before they were born.

Even the older dogs get spells of dashing hither and yon, promising one another a nice large moose or a brace of reindeer for dinner. Saxon has such a heavy coat now, he does look as if he wore a parka.

Jill says this is the time of year to reorganize everything in terms of what is oftenest used, and where it is kept. She is certainly right, and if I were an organizing person I should instantly wrestle with the jammed-up china cupboards and pack up those dishes never picked up except to dust. Also, sorting out old letters and bills, and straightening the sewing basket — Yes, this is the month to review the whole inside of the house of Stillmeadow.

Building additional shelves here and there, and then filling them up, is a February job. Though Jill often lays down the hammer to say despondently, "It isn't much good if you stand right behind me with armloads more of junk to park on them before I even get 'em painted."

The trouble is that as I pick up a cracked ironstone plate, I get to admiring the glaze and the way the edge is scalloped, and I think it is nice to look at with the candlelight glimmering on the soft finish — and back goes the plate in the same old spot.

"Have you used this in five years?" Jill says in an executive tone.

"No," I admit feebly, "but you know I might put peanuts or something in it."

"Peanuts?" says Jill.

Very often, after one of these reorganizing bouts, I will be able to pack away two chipped butter plates, one broken fork, and ten of the fifty meat skewers from the silver drawer. Then I relax with some old book that ought to be thrown out for scrap, and say happily, "Isn't it nice to get all organized before the outside work begins?"

Jill usually does not answer. She is reading seed catalogues. So I suggest brightly that she throw away all the old ones.

"I need them to refer to," she says haughtily, "to know what we planted in past years. I write in the margins."

This is the month for white sales in town, and I dare say if I were in Tahiti, I should gaze over the azure sea and say, reflectively, "I wonder what sheets are costing now?" I notice some brilliant man — or woman, probably — has finally invented sheets with tags showing what size they are. I always mean to file my sheets according to size, but they never get filed correctly. The twin size play hide and seek with me every week at Still-meadow, where we have all sizes of beds and all kinds of sheets. Flushed and unhappy, I am always lugging piles of the wrong size up and down stairs, and the worst of it is, I have a few sub-single size sheets for Donald's bed, and they creep up on me every time.

Colored sheets are enchanting, the new pale shades. I bought a pair of honey-colored ones for Cicely's room, and it is almost like sleeping in sunshine. Not that Cicely noticed it. Going to bed is an insult, she feels, that her parents impose on her nightly as some form of abuse. If she weren't the most patient, most tolerant of daughters, her attitude implies, she would go away and lead her own life. No matter what time it is, she is always in the midst of some homework that has to be handed in the next morning or she will fail. Or she is writing an editorial for the school paper, and "if it isn't handed in tomorrow, Mamma, it can't go in at all." Or she promised the Sunday School Council to get the play copied, and "Mamma, it's the most important play of the whole year. It's the only one that counts."

But poor Cicely lives from emergency to emergency. Crisis to crisis. Every meeting she attends is the most important one of the year. And the only one that matters. The whole world will rock and reel, one feels, if Cicely doesn't get to the taffy-apple fixing at Sunday school. I wish she could feel this way about mathematics, but it works in reverse for that one thing. In the rather startling jungle of Cicely's mind, mathematics is a parasitic growth on civilization's safari.

I supppose the real evidence of growing older is that things level off in importance, and instead of everything being desperately necessary, very few things are. Days are no longer jagged peaks to climb; time is a meadow, and we move over it with level steps. For me, at least, this is so. I don't expect the earth to stop turning if I miss something I have wanted. I have learned the earth rolls along.

Honey and I went to a neighbor's today. The snow was soft and fine, the air was sweet. Honey ran in the tire track, the lazy creature. She moved swiftly and lightly, making me feel like a clod. Every little while she turned and eyed me, to be sure I was still around. Funny I was so slow. When we came back it was night, and the stars were cool and immaculate, in a quiet sky. There was no sound at all except the squashing of my rubbers in the snow. The woods on either side of the road were dark and silent. It seemed as though Honey and I were the sole inhabitants of the universe. Her paws made no sound. My breathing seemed rather noisy and I held my breath as long as I could. The silence went into my bones.

Then we came near the curve and a hullabaloo burst out. The rest of the dogs, led by Star, had heard us coming. Stillmeadow sounded like circus day at Madison Square Garden. Star has a high feminine shriek. Every single cocker, in his or her own tones, announced to the world as far as Bridgeport, no doubt, that someone was coming down the road! The farm dog around the hill took up the refrain, and the whole night was musical. Honey single-footed along proudly, liking all this attention drawn to us.

On the moon-bright snow were a thousand tracks; delicate little trails here, patterned by light feet; large plumping marks there. And it looked as though little people had been dancing under the cedar tree. All the secret winter life goes

on, the rabbit and deer and the fox, the
"ol' muskrat" and the dark mink go in
and out of the meadows and woods.

Then I said over to myself a favorite
poem, which fitted the night:

   " 'Is there anybody there,' said the
      Traveller,
      Knocking on the moonlit door!"

Honey waited for me at the gate. "You
are a slow walker," she told me. "And
what are you talking about?"

"I'm saying a beautiful poem by Mr.
de la Mare," I said, "and it would benefit
you to hear it."

   "Ay, they heard his foot on the
      stirrup
      And the sound of iron on stone
      And how the silence surged softly
      backward
      When the plunging hoofs were
      gone."

My great-great-grandfather was a
minister in Boston, and among the relics
in his little haircloth, brass-studded trunk
I found this week something which

pleases me very much. I had forgotten about it during the terrible war years, and now it seems a new discovery. It is a small, yellowed box labeled "Comfort Powders." The fading, flowing script says, "Take one every morning with a generous draught of cheerfulness and thanksgiving. Good for the mind and heart, will promote love, joy, peace, long-suffering, gentleness, goodness, faith, meekness and temperance." Inside are thirty folded papers such as were used for powders by the old family doctors, folded at each end to keep the medicine from spilling. On each folded paper is a message, to be read for the day.

This is a lovely idea, I think, and bears repeating. For starting a new day with a beautiful thought might help us all. Grandfather's comfort powders were Biblical, naturally. "Peace I leave with you, my peace I give unto you: not as the world giveth, give I unto you. Let not your heart be troubled, neither let it be afraid." This is the one I like.

In a world still uneasy, these are good words to hear. And as we hear the daily news, we might feel a world of peace was a most vain illusion. But under the snow, violets sleep, and in the world there are still love, gentleness and goodness.

"Let not your heart be troubled, neither let it be afraid."

In February, after a big storm, the sun comes out with more brightness than at any other time in the year. The winter sky is pale and far-away and the snow is the essence of all the white there is. The glory of the sun with the pale sky and the white snow is breathtaking. The light has a purity, a dazzling serenity. How beautiful is the world! How fortunate we are, in spite of everything, to feel the infinite splendor of a day after a storm!

The earth begins to dream of spring. Under the brook ice the water is flowing. The long shadows on the pasture snow are violet where soon the first real violets will spread their purple. What a wondrous world we have, indeed, with the roll of the seasons, the eternal return of spring and summer.

Now, no matter how the wind piles the snowdrifts round the house, there is a different feeling about the whole business. It is a kind of second-act-curtain feeling. The third act, now coming, will be violent, fierce, catastrophic, but some of the spectators are already reaching around for dropped gloves, lost hats, and Christmas scarfs. Anyway you look at it, winter's play has a happy ending.

After Valentine's Day we can really feel that winter is on the downgrade. A few more blizzards, perhaps, but definitely March will arrive. There will be a certain day when the air comes in over the hills with a different feeling. It's an intangible thing, known only to folks who have had hard winters, and it is exciting and wonderful. One morning you poke your nose out and you know all of a sudden that there will be another spring. You smell it in the air; and no matter how deep the snow is, you think nothing of it. You dash out without your arctics and Mackinaw and catch a raging cold, but no matter — spring is coming! Tallyho!

March

Song for March

Gallops the stallion wind, unreined again
In the wild flight from winter into spring,
Tall stars are tangled in his tawny mane,
The cold moon hears his hoofbeats echoing.
Ride down the stars, oh Wind, upon your
   way,
Yours is the steeplechase whose victory
Lies in the dreamy green and tranquil day
When the rich sap makes summer of a tree.

The world is now in harness, whipped and
   checked,
And thinly measured for its pinch of dole,
Old freedoms wither, vision is suspect,
As with our fears we cramp the natural
   soul.

But being countrywise, how rich I find
The old unrationed splendor of the wind!

FOR THE WINDY month I invested in one of those sweet little string turbans with a couple of plastic pins to finish it off. In it I look like an Arab trader. All I lack is a burnoose and a camel. However, the cockers seem to accept me, turban and all, and there have been hats of mine that threw Star into hysterics. And Star could make a lot of noise!

The wind, the wild brave wind, has carried off the last of the ice and snow. How wonderful the ground looks! The sharp sunlight falls like a blade on the meadow grasses, on the brown lawn, on the huckleberry bushes in the swamp. All the browns are distinct and beautiful, and why are they different from the browns of autumn? Perhaps the new life under the bark, under the root, makes them more glowing. Perhaps it is the quality of March light, keen as an etching tool.

We often have a real blizzard in

March; but even so, we have seen the earth again and felt the wind of spring. It is just another removal sale on Nature's part.

But this lovely, brilliant light is cruel to the house. The season of mud-tracking is on us. The floors look grimy and the rugs give back a cindery crunch when you walk on them. All those ashes spread on the icy walk come right back in and lay a heavy, gritty film on everything. The windows have a natural blackout effect from furnace dust. The curtains seem to be in mild mourning.

Reason tells me I should not plan to do the real spring house cleaning unless I expect to do it all over after the furnace is cut off. If only I weren't such an emotional housekeeper! Yesterday I rushed out and removed the storm window from my front window, and washed that window. Tigger thought it an improvement, too. Now we can both see the outdoors, over the meadow, up the slope, across the old stone fence. And every hour or so a farm wagon moves across the horizon, one of them pulled by two massive white horses. What a sense of life and comfort there is in the sight of an old farm wagon creaking on a country road, the farmer drowsing on the seat, the horses moving as if they had forever to get there. After being shut away from life for so much of the winter, it is good to see movement again.

Tigger and I see the postman driving up to the box. The car is diminished by distance, but we hear the sound of the motor. He is bringing the Sears, Roebuck catalogue. Montgomery Ward, maybe. Wonderful sport, reading a mail-order catalogue. I read it in its entirety, regardless of whether the items are anything I could possibly use. The writers are so cheerful, so glowing. Not for them the gloom of news reports, the lectures on rationing. They describe their perfect wares, and if you can't get them, a simple stamp says "Not Available." But you have the fun of imagining.

In the midst of snow and sleet and rain, the shops are showing summer clothes! It's getting so you can hardly buy anything to wear at the time you need it. In summer the nice warm woollens come out for next winter, and in midwinter, the pastel sheers blossom all over town! As I trek along in galoshes and furs and mittens, I behold openwork white sandals in the windows, Mexican huaraches, beach umbrellas and, of all things, bathing suits! People who are buying such garb to go South should buy it secretly in closed rooms, I think. It's adding insult to injury for the rest of us, who brave the cold.

When I was a child, the shops faced the facts. In February the windows were still full of fleece-lined underwear and arctics. Then when the Wisconsin spring finally loosened the river ice and the logs boomed down again, out came the flowered prints. Shirts and knee-length drawers hung modestly on racks, half-hidden by lengths of crepe. A storekeeper who displayed organdy dresses in winter would have been called demented.

Slacks and shorts, of course, were unheard-of at any season. My favorite picnic costume was a starched middy and a pair of heavy serge bloomers, yards of stiff wool grabbed stoutly in under the knee with wide, strong elastics. It wasn't so long ago, either, as the crow flies.

Then there came the breath-taking day when I took Bob's old pants and hacked them off at the knee and wore them. They were a sensation, all right. The summer colony at the bay gazed at me with startled eyes, man and boy. Even the dogs were surprised. It was about this time that the full skirt came off my bathing suit, and everybody gave up wearing stockings in the water.

And now we wear slacks, sandals and halters! Or jersey sweat shirts. And I don't believe that even the fashion designers will ever get us back to the voluminous garb of yesteryear. They may get bird's nests in the hair, but they won't get long bloomers on the form. Not on my form, anyway.

Jill found an old almanac yesterday for the Year of Our Lord 1839. It was interesting reading, but very melancholy. I cannot feel that I should be cheered to read at the beginning of autumn,

"The howling of the northern blast,
Proclaims dread winter near;
Perhaps 'twill be the last,
And finish our career.

145

As for the New Year, my almanac author says cheerily,

> "How swift our fleeting moments
> fly,
> How brief is life's career;
> Thousands must end their course
> and die,
> Within the present year."

This isn't a very rollicking send-off. I prefer Arthur Guiterman's "May Song," which I find in the current almanac.

> "Above the rapids leap the trout
> In rainbow-tinted spray;
> The magazines for June are out,
> And so I know it's May."

And the modern almanac proclaims dread winter like this:

> "November nights — November
> nights —
> With all their rich and rare
> delights
> The blazing fire whose sparkling
> flames

Gleam with a lovelier light than
  Fame's!
Oh, heartful cheer, Oh, peaceful
  sights,
Walled in by cool November
  nights."

This would lead me to suppose that men have cheered up mightily since 1839. And yet the hundred years just over have been far from a golden age. Things have happened to this old world, some of them seeming to plunge us back into the gloom of the Middle Ages. The modern almanac reflects an interest in pleasantries, in playing games. I find a whole page on ski equipment, and another on planting asparagus! But I find no such sentiment as in 1839: "We know not if we shall meet again on the morrow of this year. It would be pleasant if such were our good fortune. Peradventure it may be; but again, peradventure it may not."

Of course I know joy whose finger is at his lips bidding adieu. I know beauty that must die, and I know the sadness at the heart of things. But I do not want to wallow in a whole almanacful of it. I want cheery little messages to waft me from month to month.

This is the month for another cleaning of closets and drawers, and for getting odds and ends of household repairs out of the way before the garden is ploughed. As we pack cartons with everything we can do without, to send to those who so desperately need them, I feel a small pang that we shall never have a full attic. How lovely was my grandfather's attic! But my children's children — or rather, my child's children — can never pull out old trunks full of treasures. Nobody will ever try on my black lace dress with the flounces. The quaint costumes of 1946–47 will never be used for dramatics in our family. "Grandma gave everything away," they will say.

House cleaning involves washing all the furniture with mild soap and water, and rewaxing with two thin coats of paste wax, well rubbed down. We like all our furniture finished with linseed oil and waxed.

Our method for refinishing never varies. We take off all paint and varnish with paint remover, putty knives, and coarse steel wool. I do not mean to gloss over the sweat, which is always a by-product. There is a peculiar kind of grained finish on some Connecticut antiques that resists practically everything. It is like granite to get off. But after a while we get down far enough to see the mellow wood underneath. We use fine, and then finer sandpaper toward the end, always rubbing with the grain of the wood. If you once slip, and rub crosswise, the marks are there forever. We use fine steel wool for the last half mile down. If there is a lot of dark paint residue in the grain of the wood we bleach it with a saturated solution of oxalic acid, left on overnight, then wash it thoroughly with soap and water in the morning, and rub down with steel wool again — the grade that is as soft as cotton.

When the wood is thoroughly dry, we splash on a heavy coat of turpentine and boiled linseed oil, mixed half and half. This dries in an hour and another coat goes on, until the wood has absorbed all it will hold. It is then allowed to dry overnight, or for forty-eight hours, and is polished with as many coats of wax as we have strength for. The wax must be applied in a very thin layer, and must be polished until it glows each time.

How often people say, "I can't have a cat, because I have a dog." We heard this, too. And since we had not one dog but a kennelful, we did feel doubtful at first about the advisability of adding a Siamese and a Manx.

The first time Honey saw Tigger, she froze instantly, her eyes large as plates. She stared, and even stopped breathing. Tigger stared back, also not breathing. At the time he was a mere kitten, ink-black and snub-nosed and with clear, translucent yellow-green eyes.

For a good half hour the two stood, staring. Now and then a whisker quivered, and that was all. Finally I got nervous and moved Honey away. She went backward, head turned over her shoulder, still staring.

Tigger eyed her retreat, lifted a paw, and gave it a lick. Spaniels were nothing to bother a man, he indicated, inspecting a paw.

Then Sister came in, and began to prance around, wagging her rear end almost off. "Oh, goody, goody, a nice surprise Mamma brought us," she said. She made a sportive dash at the cat, and out whipped the indolent paw. Sister fell back in amazement.

"Prickers!" she said, "the thing wears prickers!"

Irrepressibly she hopped up again. Fire and smoke greeted her. "Here's a funny thing," she said, and sat down thoughtfully. All day she had moments of wanting to try again, and made sudden sallies from under the bed, or around the sofa.

By the next day, Tigger was in control of the household.

Our back kitchen used to be a rendezvous for all the best mice in Connecticut. We keep the dehydrated dogfood there, and they love it. The condition of our mice, and yes, rats, used to be a fine advertisement for our brand of food.

They would never touch the nonpoisonous-to-animals rat poison. They paid no attention to wire cages, or steel wool stuffed in cracks. A trap meant nothing to them.

But the advent of the cats changed all that. A great silence descended in the back kitchen, and the woodshed too. The first few days, Tigger had rather severe indigestion; the hunting was too good.

Cats are so independent; when they feel in a hunting mood, they go to the door and rake it with lifted paw. The door opens, they slide through. Tigger leaps to the shelf and Esmé perches on the thin edge of the sink. The back kitchen is theirs.

Now we haven't a spaniel on the place that would voluntarily scratch at any door to get out and do something on his or her own. All the scratching they do — and it is plenty — is to get on the same side of the door that we are on. If they were going to do any hunting in the back kitchen, they would wait until I went out there with them. If I left to do something, they would abandon everything and leave instantly.

Therefore, if we ever had a spaniel who caught mice, it would involve my sitting by the mousehole myself, reading a good book while the cocker hunted.

Nothing makes a house cosier than cats. And nothing looks so comfortable as a cat. If a person is nervously exhausted, a cat would be the best prescription I know of. Just looking at the long, fluent line of the relaxed body is restful, and the lovely incredible smoothness of movement when a cat leaps from the floor to the dresser gives the onlooker a sensation of vicarious lightness and ease. Just as when I see a good ballet, I come home positive that I can float around like thistledown myself.

Fundamentally, however, I am all cocker. Much as I admire and respect cat nature, I just haven't got it. I think like a spaniel, and I, too, am forever trying to get on the same side of the door with what I love.

It would surprise anyone who didn't know Siamese cats to see how perfectly Esmé knows the different personalities of ten cockers. She is perfectly willing to cuddle down with Honey on the couch, but she wouldn't stay near Melody. She feels Melody is too childish and irresponsible. She and Silver chase each other all over the house, knocking down bric-a-brac and skidding over the rugs, but she never plays ball with Saxon. She as much as says Sister and Clover are all right, but not very exciting, and Windy is a wolf.

When Tigger and Esmé begin to play basketball, some of the cockers think it is pretty silly. Hildegarde wishes to play too. Melody will step right in and get cuffed for it. Honey is bored to extinction.

By March, Tigger is a lot of cat. He is the blackest Manx, and the biggest, and in winter he lets his hunting slide a little. It is too cold to racket around after mice in the barn, he feels; he'd rather lie on the radiator. When he thinks he should eat, he stretches and yawns and moves to the kitchen, sits down by the stove and waits. If he is ignored he draws attention to the clock by uttering faint, pitiful wails. It sounds as though every wail were the last breath he could draw in this alien world, but he keeps on until his dinner is put down. Then he gives a few resounding purrs and begins to eat.

Of course, at Stillmeadow we don't hunt for hobbies — we have so many we never catch up with them. And just as we think we are more or less settled down, we start something new and exciting and we are off again, like hunters after a fox.

For instance, milk glass. We have a

dear friend who was suffering a great grief. She found herself in a desperate state, as we all do at times. So she sat down one day, after a sleepless night, and said, "Now look here, you have got to stop thinking only about this, and about yourself. It's time you did something." She had a short vacation from her job at the time, but family duties kept her confined to the city. "All right," she said, "I'll just collect something." So she spent her vacation wandering in little shops, and riding busses and street cars to remote second-hand stores, and going to the library to read about milk glass. Now she has a beautiful collection of glass; but more, she learned the value of a lively interest in some external things. "Whenever I got too low," she said, "I tried to match the blackberry creamer."

We didn't need to have our minds taken from anything personal at that moment, but we saw the milk glass she had, and it conquered. And now our own modest collection keeps us in a constant fever of excitement. There is really something amazing to collecting. Going into a dusty, grimy junk shop and seeing two one-o-one plates, for instance, just waiting to come home and be loved. Finding a blackberry egg cup in Roxbury and another just like it in Brooklyn.

Somehow, since the war has destroyed so much beauty, I hope many people will begin to save and love the old things that are left, to cherish and preserve whatever is available. It is good for us to keep our roots in the past, just as we draw so much strength and courage from great men and women who have lived before our time. Change is a fine thing; growth is necessary in our ideas, our institutions and our way of life. And yet I think we should be very careful not to become a regimented people, and not to discard the value of individuality.

Whatever wisdom we have in the next generation will come from around the supper table, not the political halls, or the state houses. The woman who brings in the pot roast, and father who carves it and complains that the knife is not sharp, and the children who talk about what the history course in school is like — this is the real cradle of government. This is the great job for every woman who has her family around her.

This is a good time of year for parties. Friendship glows brightly when the fire burns clear and comfortable upon the hearth.

We decided last week to have a big party and ask twice as many people as the house will hold. After much thought, we decided to have a come-and-go party, serving a buffet dinner from five-thirty to eight-thirty.

Jill said, "But they'll all come at once, and stay the whole night."

I felt optimistic about the ones with young children to get to bed. "We ought to make it plain it is a special kind of supper," I said. "Why don't we call it a hunt supper?"

"What are we hunting for?" asked Jill, in astonishment.

"Well, we'll just call it open house," I said, giving up my flight of fancy.

"If they all come at once, it will be open house all right," prophesied Jill. "The walls will fall outward."

There is a hazard about a party in February, but it is well worth facing. If a bad blizzard comes, the poles may go down, or the wires break, and the house be plunged into darkness. Often we have had the chicken roasting, the pie nearly done, and the guests plowing to the door just as the current went off. It is an excellent lesson in the helplessness of too-civilized people. For nothing is deader than a dead electric stove. Meanwhile, the electric stoker on the furnace stops too, and the water pump sits idly on its belt, so there will be no water in half an hour. By now the phone is as useful as an Egyptian mummy, and the nervous members of the family begin to wring their hands and say, "The freezer will thaw! All the food will spoil!"

Winter! But we build up the fire in the old faithful range and add great logs to the fireplaces, and light the candles, and carry in water from the unelectric neighbor's spring. Some of our gayest parties have been given at such a time, when the guests help themselves in the glow of the tall ivory candles to the tender, sizzling chicken (which did get done on the range), and toast rolls over the open fire. The radio and phonograph being voiceless, the company can sing, and tell favorite stories.

Even a waffle breakfast can be managed. Though I really felt qualms when I was trying to do waffles for a brace of lanky, hungry Army lieutenants on the electric waffle iron and the current blanked out. One waffle glued itself to the grids with a death grip and the boys came rolling out with empty plates and expectant smiles.

"Boy, it's nice and peaceful here," they said.

Hastily I carried the remains of the batter to the faithful wood range and said, "How about pancakes for a change?"

The old soapstone griddle we found in the house when we bought it makes the best pancakes in the world. It really holds its own against the electric waffle iron.

For a come-and-go party the best food is a ham, sliced thin, and thinly sliced turkey or roast chicken. We do the turkey or chickens the week before and freeze it. Freeze the light rolls, too, and the cake. Then thaw and heat and serve when ready. There are the casseroles left, and they are simple. If you make small ones, you may keep taking out a fresh, hot one, rich with steamy flavor.

My favorite is a macaroni dish, made with the Italian shell-shaped macaroni, boiled until tender, placed in a deep casserole with plenty of mushrooms, butter, salt and pepper, frozen or canned whole-kernel corn, slivers of cheese and a diced green pepper. I use top milk for the liquid, or mushroom soup which has been slightly thinned.

This casserole is perfect with any kind of fish or chicken.

A seafood casserole is delicious too. Oysters, shrimp, salmon, tuna laid in a heavy cream sauce, topped with buttered crumbs and baked. Cole slaw makes a good salad to accompany this, and you can make it early in the day. We add diced pineapple to ours, and grate carrots on top. I always put herbs in the dressing, too.

On these icy mornings we like a good breakfast. I think with nostalgia of the breakfasts of the early Americans who lived in this house. I know what they had; they had pie! Good, robust, flaky, rich, spicy apple pie. Aside from this they ate only ham, eggs, pickles, cheese, sausage, pancakes and sirup and, for Sunday, codfish balls.

I remember I loved to visit my grandmother in West Springfield, for we always had meat and potatoes and pie for breakfast. Wheatcakes, too. At my Aunt Grace's we had creamy delicate golden-brown codfish balls every Sunday, and Uncle Walter had a pot of leftover baked beans from Saturday night. Then we had cereal, too, of course, piles of hot toast and coffee with thick cream frosting it.

At home we had a "light" breakfast. Papa and I had big bowls of hot cereal with brown sugar and cream. Then we never had anything else except eggs and bacon or thin fried ham, or waffles and maple sirup, or wheatcakes. Hot blueberry muffins in season. If the meal was too slim, Papa went out in the kitchen and fried a big panful of potatoes with onion to supplement it. We all drank four cups of coffee, and we were the healthiest family I ever saw.

Jill and I order just a few more berry bushes, fruit trees, and roses; it isn't too late. Jill reads dreamily, "The fruit is sweet and juicy enough to eat when it is

161

only half ripe. The catalogue says so. In the golden stage. Continue to eat and enjoy it until September, when the skin is rich maroon red and the flesh is tempting gold."

"What is it?" I ask.

"Kind of a peach and plum and apricot all mixed up," she says. "It is delightful canned."

"Get one," I say. I never resist the lure of anything that may be canned.

Jill reads on: "The originator removes one third to one half the crop every year to keep trees from breaking down under the load of fruit. When properly thinned, the fruit becomes so large it must be canned in halves."

Just once I should like to see one tree on our land that had enough fruit to break down a branch. Or even to shatter a small twig. But I am always as hopeful as Jill. You never know when the seed catalogue's dream may come true. After all, we had three plums this year.

Of course, the catalogues never take into account such things as we have to cope with. All their trees and berries grow in some Elysian field, where age does not wither them, nor scale nor blight nor curculio enter in. No rabbits eat their apricot trees just as they get their feet firm in the ground. No cows get in and step largely among the tender berry shoots. No horse, certainly no horse, ever dances back and forth on their strawberry patch, eating all the mulch and bashing all the berries. The roses and lilies bloom in serenity, also. There are no puppies scrambling back and forth through the iris beds, no golden boys tiptoeing through the tulips.

No, in the catalogues there is only flowering perfection and there are only flawless fruits. So we read all the catalogues eagerly, and plant once more, which is an annual experiment, an annual thrill. In the end, we have marvelous vegetables and plenty of lovely flowers, a handful or two of berries, and one pear. So we should feel satisfied.

As far as the cockers are concerned, this is the month of mud. The puppies, Melody and Silver, and Hildegarde, love best of all to smoosh around in the mud a while and then bounce up in my arms because they feel good and it's going to be spring. Wild licking and wagging and squirming and whoofing, as if they never could bear being so ecstatic. Too small a cocker is, to carry so much love. Silver and Snow give a couple of affectionate leaps in passing and then whirl away like blowing gold and dark leaves.

Silver flashes to the front gate to see if there isn't someone coming that she can bark at and tell off in no uncertain terms. And maybe she can see Shep, the German police dog belonging to George across the road. Then she can jump up and down and carry on like a soap-box orator. What she thinks of police dogs! Shep is very polite and always rambles over to cock a thoughtful listening ear on the other side of the picket fence.

Clover greets me and tears back to the swamp side of the house where the big rabbit lives. Who knows — he might just happen to be inside and ready for fun.

But Sister is the sweet one. Whenever I let her out of the kennel, she always runs back three times and jumps against me and says thank you. No matter how tempting is the prospect outside, Sister comes back just to be sure I know how grateful she is. Now that Sister is getting older, I often seem to get a curious lump in my throat when she does this. Her eager lifted face looks up at me so earnestly, so bright with love.

Honey sits on the terrace keeping her golden feet nice and dry. Saxon doesn't care how muddy it is, and there is so much of him, and he is so blond!

Snow looks the worst, because her white is so very white, and her hair so soft a texture that the mud gives her the look of a wet mop. I try not to wash her until she can stay clean at least a day or so. She has nice long petticoats, and they make a snowy fringe after she is laundered. She stands proudly waiting to be brushed out; I suspect Snow of being on the vain side about her looks. But Snow is almost too good, as a matter of fact. She is so gentle and unselfish and reliable and anxious to make everyone happy. I always feel apologetic that she cannot go to the Red Cross and roll bandages every afternoon. And she is just the kind of girl who would peel the potatoes for the church supper, and wash the pots and pans afterward.

Esmé does not care for wind, or damp earth either. She stays in the sunniest window, looking out and keeping her fur dry. Summer nights are for Esmé and Tigger, when it is hot and still, and they can go wild in the moonlight.

Esmé catches a mouse now and then. It is always a very small, very special mouse. She seems to feel a little doubtful about the propriety of a Royal Siamese engaging in mousing. She reminds me of Marie Antoinette milking a cow in her imitation rustic village on the grounds of Versailles. But when she brings her mouse in, she comes with long, beautiful leaps in the air. She rises completely above the law of gravity, and the mouse rises with her!

A cat has so much imagination. A cat invents a whole drama around a mouse; a cat is, by and large, sophisticated and complex, and capable of creating three-act plays around any single piece of action. Also, at least *our* cats have a drive that cockers lack. You can talk a cocker out of something, but not a cat. Esmé and Tigger both feel confident that they are always right, and the best thing for their humans to do is fall in line with them and not waste energy trying to reason.

When the house is all cleaned, I like to shut the door and climb the hill across the brook. The March wind seems to be blowing winter down the valley. The world, too, or at least my New England, has had a spring cleaning.

The brook is filled with dark water and tears down the hill at my feet. The little sandy places have gleams of garnet red and gold. What a marvelous mystery sand is, I think. I pick up a handful.

If I think about the vastness of time that has passed to make this shining sand, how much less than one grain is my whole life span! I feel the wing of eternity brush my face for an instant. And then I climb back down the hill, rather hastily, for the reassuring sight of Stillmeadow.

A bevy of muddy spaniels waits to rush in and swarm over those clean floors. Sister is ready to make nests in all the slip covers and throw all the pillows on the floor and wallow in them. Saxon has dug up a particularly fearsome bone and has every idea of playing games with it in the front living room.

I mean to be firm, unpleasant; and

then I think of that handful of sand and suddenly I know the house was meant to be lived in, day by day, and every day should be full of love and laughter as long as we can keep it so. I open the door and we all burst in together.

"How about a snack?" suggests Saxon hopefully.

April

Song for April

Once more the winter night reluctantly
Draws back her tides along the shore of
     spring,
The drift lies fugitive upon the lea
In foam, and whiter snow the snowdrops
     bring,
Presaging summer's full security.
The brook unbound makes silver
     murmuring,
Rosy the flowers on the maple tree
And in the swamp at night the hylas sing.

This is the proof, this April testament
That from the dark earth springs the secret
     seed
Instinct with life; this is the sacrament
Which manifests God's answer to man's
     need.

Tell me no more that loss endures, or pain,
When lilacs bud along the country lane.

APRIL IS THE month when the youngest puppies come out in the spring sun. They live in the warm dry kitchen in a play pen until the danger of colds is past, and now they have their first walk on the green grass. We carry them out and put them down. "My goodness, what have we here?" they ask. They move tentative paws, they sniff the grass, they begin to wag their fat little selves, they stagger around in dizzy circles of joy. Then they make silly lunges at one another, growling almost as loud as a mouse. When you pick them up, they snuggle in your neck, and make squeaks of joy, and polish you thoroughly with baby flannel tongues. And all the time they wiggle. Cocker puppies are simply bursting with joy from the minute they are born.

We have done a good deal of talking this spring about training Melody and Hildegarde and Silver. We saw the Obedience Trials at the Spaniel Specialty

Show and our consciences were smitten by the idea that our own darlings were growing up like hoodlums. Rip and Sister are the only perfectly trained cockers we have ever raised. There was nothing Rip could not have learned except to cook roast beef. He would have had to taste the roast. He would retrieve over an obstacle, heel, and do figure eights without a lead, sit motionless while Jill walked away, and hold his pose until she called.

The hardest thing to teach a cocker is to stay while you walk away. Heeling is fine because you do that together, but when you get about two paces away from your darling, there is a mad scramble, and she flings herself at you, saying wildly, "You didn't really mean you were going to leave me *alone?*" Most cockers train very quickly to the leash. Even Melody leads very well now that she has gotten over the habit of lying down on her back and waving her paws helplessly in the air the minute the collar goes on.

Spring puppies and spring plowing! Of all the farm processes, I think plowing moves me most. Of course, by August I shall begin to feel that harvesting is the thing. We wait and watch for days for the ground to dry out, the weather to be just right. And then, one clear sunny morning, George comes in with a smile to say, "I'll plow the garden today; I'm doing the upper meadow anyhow. Ground's all right."

We stop whatever we are doing and rush outside to watch the great plow ride along, turning the dark furrows, turning the good earth, turning the rich soil. It is a tie between us and our forefathers; it is something we inherit with the land itself. It is always new and always old. The blades of the plow are silver in the sun as the earth breaks from the sterile grasp of winter and folds back. George rides the plow, and he looks beautiful to me with his farm shirt open and the sun on his face and his blue eyes smiling.

We have been all over Mr. Faulkner's book about not plowing, and Mr. Bromfield's and Mr. Ed Robinson's too. Jill is a fiend for Keeping Up with Modern Trends. And I fear it is really due to my romantic feelings that we go on in the old-fashioned way, plowing the garden. But I point out to the family that we have crops out of this world, anyway; carrots a foot long and tender as butter, elegant crisp celery, rich tight lettuce. So why not go on plowing?

At last the storm windows are off. I usually begin thinking about taking them off the first nice warm day in February. But the more sane members of the family point out that in New England there are blizzards even in March, and the old glass in the little-paned windows may be beautiful, but doesn't keep out the wind very well.

Last fall when the windows went on, they had been freshly painted and all the identifying numbers painted over. Every window in the house is a different size, but not different enough for the naked eye to measure. So, on a day when it was below zero, one of those sudden drops to remind us of winter, Jill and George and I ran round and round the house with windows, none of which ever fitted anywhere. It was like one of those maddening puzzles enlarged to life size. I dare say most families don't have difficulties like this. Further, the windows hook inside as well as out, and all the inner hooks are at differing levels. This involves someone's running in and out of the house and rabbiting around and back, hooking and unhooking again.

But now it's spring again, and the storm windows are a problem of the past. I must remember this year to have them all numbered. They should be stored resting upright on boards so the sash has air circulation around it. They should never be dumped in a damp cellar with the sill on the floor. Storm windows rot and warp, no matter how sturdy they look.

Tigger and Esmé hate to see the screens go on. They like best to go in and out through my bedroom windows; and when the storm windows are on and half open, they have their own entrance at night. When the screens are on, they must go in the door like ordinary people. Cats are the most individual, I sometimes think, of all our friends. Esmé always drinks water from a flower bowl, when she has a perfectly good dish of water on the floor. She buries her little wedge face in the flowers after I have them all arranged according to my best idea, and laps daintily. The flowers are rearranged by courtesy of the Siamese.

The cellar at Stillmeadow is very romantic and pleasing, and entirely impractical. But I like to look at the heavy, hand-hewn beams and the great stones of the fourteen-foot-square chimney, and the old rough wall stones as I work at clearing out and rearranging the fruit shelves, even if I sometimes wish I had enough shelves and cupboard space to keep the place neat and tidy. We spray the stone with casein paint in the spring if we get time, and that helps.

And maybe our cellar would never be much to look at. We do so many things there, especially in winter. Right now it is full of Jill's mushroom bed, a chest of drawers in the process of being done over, three window boxes with pails of earth and sand and fertilizer around them, and fishing boots, and the plumber's overalls and a couple of navy caps the dogs brought in, we know not from where.

Raising mushrooms is not too difficult when you give in to it. Jill uses a large square wooden packing box which we had for our books when we went to college. The former house for William

James and Kant and *Twelve Centuries of English Literature* is now the happy home of mushrooms, and I think it does very well.

To grow mushrooms you must fill your bed at least twelve inches deep with fresh horse manure, the straw bedding included. A thermometer is necessary, for you turn the bed every two weeks until the temperature has dropped to 55–60°F. This takes about six weeks. After that you must try to maintain it at the same temperature. The spawn is planted, and when it begins to "run" — white threads appear — you case the bed with rich loam to a depth of two inches. You keep the bed damp, but not wet. The first time we had ours too wet, and no mushrooms ever appeared. The mushrooms start coming in six to eight weeks and continue for from eight to ten weeks, and then you begin over again. The spawn comes in liquid or brick form. There is really a wonderful satisfaction in running down to the cellar and picking half a pound of fresh mushrooms, silvery white and perfect; and like everything else in the food world, fresh ones are simply elegant.

You have to think of that while the cellar smells like a stable. This odorous state does not last long, however.

Honey and I always go up to see the dogtooth violets and the delicate spring beauties. I love the violets best. The tawny gold of the flower and the delicate striping on the long narrow leaves and the cool slender little stem are all so exquisite and so beautiful. I pick the violets and feel their coolness and see their carved pointed leaves, and I know all over again that the tramp of nailed boots on the good earth is going to stop.

Faith is a curious thing. It must be renewed; it has its own spring. The dogtooth violets have a brief span. They will soon be gone and the hillside carpeted with summer green. But here they are now, and next spring they will come again, and there is a meaning in this for all sick and weary folk.

I had a strange wish yesterday. I wish the men who are going to form the peace for the world would all have to come to this spot, and jump across the free-running brook where the sand lies golden under the amber water, and climb this little obscure country hill and just stand awhile on the violet-covered slope. I would ask them not to say any fine brave words about peace and the new world, nor to make those glittering promises I hear over the radio from them all, that have no real bones under the oratory.

None of them, for a little time, would be politicians or dictators, or world rulers. I would ask them to smell the quiet air and listen to the tranquil country sounds; the dog after a rabbit, the first birds pricking the stillness with sweet voices, the thunder of a horse in his stall at the next farm, the bark of a fox near Kettletown.

I would ask them to remember when they were children and believed in life. Power and expansion and new territories and national glory would mean nothing at all. They would be just a group of middle-aged men.

Maybe they would pick a few golden violets and see the wonder of what God makes, just sort of casually and for nothing!

Then they might walk down the hill in the April dusk and begin their world machinery by saying to one another,

"How shall we save the world for simple people? How shall we make sure that all men may have their hearths, and their children pick flowers in the springtime?"

This suffering that we have endured brims the cup of the world. Somehow it must be justified. It might be, if the world rulers will think first of love for men and afterward of all the technical problems.

I have been reading Kahlil Gibran, since the new book about him came out. I like what he said: "How shall my heart be unsealed unless it be broken?"

In the dusk, coming across the fields with Honey, carrying the yellow violets, I said the words aloud to myself, and felt hope for a better world.

"How shall my heart be unsealed unless it be broken?"

Jill is going over the fishing tackle to see that it is ready for the season, which opens this month. I have a new, splendid bait-casting rod from a friend in Virginia, sent with a firm note: "This is for you to learn to cast with." My previous attempts at casting have been startling. First I caught two bushes and the seat of Jill's breeches. Then I got my own neck. Finally I was embroiled in a birch tree. I wonder if it would work better if I turned my back to the water and cast off behind me. I always seem to get something tangible in the rear.

Then another thing. I like to catch fish, even very small fish. And standing on the bank of Eight Mile Brook, dropping a simple worm as bait, I can be sure of getting at least a mud turtle or a salamander. But when you cast expertly, I understand you get either a real game fish or nothing. For me a sunfish in the hand is worth ten trout in the water. So I expect that Jill and Don can go on playing games with their rods, while I bring home the bullheads. Eight Mile Brook is my dish. I know it's chiefly occupied by turtles and water spiders, but it is so beautiful. It gives me a sense of release just to stand at the bend and look up the stream.

After all, catching something is purely a by-product of our fishing. It is the act of fishing that wipes away all grief, lightens all worry, dissolves fear and anxiety. Why this is, I don't know. But when you fish, you simply forget all the world. No thought of dinner or supper or unpaid bills mars the surface of the water. The only thing of import is a small cork, generally lying tranquil on the bosom of the stream.

When the fishing season opens, garden or no garden, we have to rig up the reels and get out the tackle box. Trout fishing has begun. All the nearby streams look as if they were the center of an Elks' convention. We can hardly see the water for the fishermen.

We have very nice waders, although it is a fact that I can hardly walk in mine. We can all, by now, cast very nicely when we bait-cast for pickerel; or bass. But to date we have never caught a trout. The art of flicking a fly and actually getting a fish on it is a complicated one. Trout just aren't ingenuous. Sometimes I wonder if they ever get hungry, with a real natural appetite.

The Pomperaug is running strongly now, with white water around the curves. The sweet, fresh smell of spring is in the air, and the sound of birds, which I can't identify because my hook is caught on a willow.

The veteran trout fishermen come up

softly on the bank, letting no shadow fall on the water. I can't help it; I have to laugh when I see them. They look like Christmas Day before the presents are opened. They are hung at every conceivable spot with creels and tackle boxes and rods, and their hats are stuck full of flies. Landing nets hang limp from their middles, and their faces are radiant.

Jill was upstream with her back turned, when one expert made a perfect cast, and his fly caught Jill in the middle of her shirt. "You'll never get a bigger trout than that," said his companion happily, as Jill came back and the poor man unhooked her.

This was a pleasant introduction, so we fell into talk. Most real fishermen are friendly and kind to novices. I think they are a good breed of men, like the doggy men. These two gave us some extra live bait they weren't using and suggested we try in certain deep holes the trout love.

And we all talked about The Trout. This Trout has lived in a special hole near the rude bridge that arches the flood, and he has been there since time immemorial. Nobody can catch him. Everything known to man has been offered to him:

dry flies, wet flies, natural nymph creepers, beetles, grasshoppers.

"Probably some boy will get him with a worm," said one of the men.

We all crept up on the bridge and lay on our stomachs and looked down. There in the shadowy depths he lay, perfectly visible, a king in his own right. I would, of course, give practically anything to be the one to catch him; and yet, at the same time, I kept hoping he never would be caught. My emotions are always getting underfoot in this irrational way.

"I come over every week during the season and spend a day on him," said the second man wistfully.

"He's not going to bite today," the other assured him, "come on down to the riffles."

Jill said, "A boy got a big pickerel in that side water yesterday."

"Funny about pickerel," said the first man. "I saw a swampy pool right in the middle of a cornfield the other day as I was going across to trout water. There was an old hick countrywoman in blue jeans and with a felt hat, standing there and just whanging down on the water with a bamboo pole. So I asked her what for, and she said she was catching herself a pickerel. I said, 'You can't get pickerel here, lady,' and she said she could. Whang, she went. She'd lift that old pole with both hands and come down like a brickbat with it." He laughed. "Next thing I knew she came up with a pickerel big as your arm. She put him under her arm and started away. She said, 'Every day I get a pickerel here. Every day I catch one and the Lord sends another one.' I figured she must make 'em so mad whanging at 'em, that they bite out of pure rage. But what they're doing in the cornfield I wouldn't know."

"Pickerel's a peculiar fish," asserted the other as they left us. "True enough, one always comes back to take the place of a caught one." They waved at us and waded downstream with a final, "Let us know if you catch the Old One!"

Shadows were falling on the water. We had a few fair strikes and no fish. I knelt to take a last look at the Old One, secure and royal in his twilight pool. The water was clear amber now, darkened with the evening light. Overhead the sky was tinged with pale, pale apricot, and the banks were still and dark.

185

Don packed up the tackle. Wading in the swift icy water is hard work, and the footing none too easy to maintain. Water dripped from Jill's waders as she climbed out. Don was dumping his worms in the coffee can now. He fishes with worms for everything.

We took the suspiciously light creels and started home. True, we had no trout. We had some hours spent in the spring woodlands, we had friendly talk with some fellow men. We had the sight of the Old One moving a fin.

"Didn't we have a wonderful time," said Don happily.

"Perfect," said Jill.

"And now for supper," said Don, "You said we'd have fish tonight."

"So we shall," I said placidly, "crab soufflé."

Sometimes I think that when Pandora opened the fateful box and all the evils poured out, and then she withdrew the one blessing, hope, what she really pulled from the box was April. For April is hope. The last snow melting in the hollows, the roads running with cold, clear water, the brook leaping over its winter bounds, and the whole world changing mysteriously, a white-and-brown world to a world misted with green.

April means the planting of early vegetables, the maples budding, and the garden ready for another season. We always plant very early and often have some things nipped; but the residue comes in so far ahead of the later plantings that we don't mind. Every year we have learned something about varieties, their resistance to pests and disease, the texture and characteristics that make for quality. Jill makes notes in the seed catalogues, so that each year we approach nearer to a perfect garden.

I personally enjoy planting onion seed. We put in seed, and then sets, and more sets and seed, so that we have a succession planting of onions the whole season, and plenty to store for winter. I am passionately devoted to onions. I don't think we should have enough if we planted the whole forty acres to onions. But then there are edible-podded peas, and the lettuce, and tomatoes — there's a vegetable they should have eaten on Olympus instead of ambrosia. I plant onion seeds while Don gets in the peas and Jill is communing with the new raspberry bushes.

As I straightened my stiff back and lifted my face to the warm sun this morning, it suddenly came over me that we have a plan! I've mourned often that we were all so lacking in organization as far as the garden is concerned that we never made scale drawings or kept files or had indexes. Jill has a masterful index for the kennel, and I do keep my recipes in a blue enamel box. But a real magazine-like plan for the garden we have never had. But suddenly I realized that we have a very good plan, for us. This is our plan: to increase the berry bushes and the perennial crops like asparagus; to bring to bearing enough fruit trees for eating and for my beloved fruit closet and freezing unit; to plant the vegetables we have tested and that we know can and freeze successfully, and finally, to develop as many perennial shrubs and flowers as possible to save time and labor, and then to grow our special, favorite annuals as God wills.

Now this is practical for any family of five or six, I should think. In time we hope to raise everything we need except meat, and still have time to go fishing.

Now and then we speak tentatively again of raising chickens, but the problem of who would kill the ones to be eaten always ends the discussion. Jill has a phobia against birds of any kind, due, she explains, to a bad chicken bite received in infancy. Bob's father once raised fancy show chickens, and he remembers how hard it was to keep them clean. The idea of using our own eggs, gathered in our own basket, moves me romantically, but I draw back at the killing business.

But I am almost persuaded toward a cow. Jill yearns over cows. And a cow is practically the only beast I am not *en rapport* with. To me, a cow is definitely a wild animal. I base this on a certain roll of the eyes whenever I am near a cow, which is seldom. But the chicken woman has a small soft brown cow that looks more amiable. It has rather the color and expression of a deer. So eventually I expect a cow will be found whose face has enough appeal for me to accept her. Jill assures me that the facial expression is not the most vital part of a cow, but I am adamant. I want a cow that looks tame.

I know of nothing to compare with the welcome a dog gives you when you come home. If I go to the village for half an hour, I am welcomed with a regular silver jubilee on my return. And there's never any reproach for my having gone. None of the "Well, I thought you never would get back; you certainly were gone a long time — we nearly gave you up." Only joyful excitement as the spaniels say, "How marvelous you are! Look, she's back again! Let's celebrate!" They act as if I had done them an incredible favor by coming home. It gives me a sense of richness, and a lovely thankfulness that I could come home. And when I am sad, I begin to worry about how they shall be comforted when I go down the road someday and don't come back.

With mixed feelings I report that my birthday is this month. How I used to pray for it to arrive; there was a special glory in having my own day, not to mention my own presents. I suppose anyone who loves things as much as I do likes a gift day. Elegant smooth bath soap, fragrant sea-colored bath salts, new country-smelling perfume. Gadgets, I love them. And yet, as the birthdays move along, I feel sometimes they come down rather more like the wolf on the fold than like fairies bearing garlands of poesy. Presently I shall look on my birthday presents as consolation prizes.

Birthday presents should be special and personal, I think. The real test of a birthday gift is that it suits the one person, and no one else. Just the right book is better than a diamond bracelet, if you like books. A piece of Mexican glass, or a vase that is right for gladioli, or a plain wooden bowl for salad — these are the kinds of gifts. And a birthday letter is fine.

It was tradition when I was a child that on my birthday all my favorite food was served. This meant generally a waffle breakfast: golden-crisp waffles with real maple sirup and tender broiled bacon. Then I had the pleasant ordeal of deciding what to have for dinner and supper. Steak. New England fried chicken (we ate it in Wisconsin, but it was New England just the same), baking powder biscuits. Or roast beef with the good crusty outside piece for me, and plenty of light dumplings and gravy. I was lukewarm about salad, but I wanted fried tomatoes; perhaps I ought to ask for fried tomatoes with cream gravy for supper, red sizzling disks, and the gravy poured over the platter so the brown butter and extra red juice mixed with the smooth cream in flavor — what a flavor! Apple pie, sizzling too, and with the top crust lifted while three inches of whipped cream was spread under it. There was a dish, and nobody counted calories. Or Lady Baltimore cake. There was a birthday cake, too, angel food with pink candles on it.

Quite often I felt less good the next day, but it was worth it. Almonds and peanuts cracked at home, blanched, and browned in pans of butter and salt in a hot oven, filled up any cracks left after the rest of the meals.

Cicely has made a scrapbook of her favorite poems. Last night we got to reading them aloud, and I wished that I had saved my favorites when I was endowed with more leisure than I have now. Cicely had "A Song of Senlin" by

Conrad Aiken, which I had never known:

"It is evening, Senlin says, and in
   the evening
   By a silent shore, by a far distant
   sea,
   White unicorns come gravely
   down to the water."

I am going to remember those lines always. Magic like this cannot be analyzed; it is there, evoking the very image of beauty. I made a resolve to memorize something every day, storing up bits of beauty in my mind where I can get at them. Poetry is a refuge for the soul. Cicely did not have my own "Lonely Unicorn," and it belongs here too:

"Ascending through the twilit wood,
   Slowly he rose and strangely stood
   In the dark silver of the trees
   Mane trailing mosses to his knees—"

Surely, I thought, if I went over the hill in the old orchard, I might see a white unicorn myself, come grave and silent along the singing brook. But it takes a stout heart to look at one, because you are changed. It is like looking at Deirdre in a green Irish wood, or following La Belle Dame Sans Merci. You must be very careful with the world of faery.

I myself shall never give up my belief in the little people. It is perfectly easy to believe in things you don't see, if you have a little imagination and don't curb it too harshly. And I like to think the moonlit woods around Stillmeadow have magic in them. I am sure they have.

Running a more-or-less farm with practically no help takes a lot of ingenuity to replace real strength. I stand bemused when I see our farm neighbor pick up a hundred-pound sack of dog food as if it were a pack of cigarettes. You have to be born and bred on the land to have this easy strength with material things. It is a fine thing. To watch the farm boys cut a dead, massive walnut, as we did last fall, is to see poetry. The sweep of arms, the flash of the saw, the blade of the ax, the sonnet of chips falling exactly from the center, and at last the epic grandeur of the crash — this lifts the heart.

The trouble with this month is there isn't enough of it. The lawn has to be cleaned up, rolled and, alas, mowed. The house has its final spring cleaning, whatever was left over from last month. Now all our sins of omission rest on us; those lawn chairs we failed to repair, the screens we didn't get painted. We feel like jugglers. The kennel runs must be raked clean, and limed or salted or both, and left to sun. The kennels get a thorough scrubbing and disinfecting, and the floors are oiled again. All the tools must be wiped free of grease and the handles painted. A nice quiet life in the country.

But there is something exciting about it. The nights are cool and the peepers cry from the swamp; the sweetest music there is, to me. The days have wine in the air, and the sun has spilled all over the border in daffodils. And when we sit briefly on the terrace, rubbing bruised knees and inspecting blistered hands, we smell the growing things, and hear the brook running swift.

A cold spell — and a film of ice covers the ponds and lakes. A neighbor came in to say the wild ducks flew over night before last, and couldn't find water to come down on. He opened his door and listened, and heard the wild ducks crying as they went round and round looking for water. The edge of the river was the only resting place.

Wild ducks crying in a spring night. I wish I had heard them.

I did see robins. A whole flock of them flashing over the brown hills. What a comforting sight for winter-weary folk, the sturdy, cheerful robins! They were all busy and didn't mind the cold.

And a song sparrow woke me up at dawn with a cool, liquid note. It sounded like spring itself. I think, though, that the sweetest sound in spring is the first soft piping from the marshes, when the hylas begin. In the spring night the sound of the peepers comes through my window, and it seems as if life is beginning all over again for the whole barren earth.

Spring is always a surprise to me. It never seems possible that this is the same yard that was knee-deep in snow and armored in ice. Suddenly it is starred with daffodils, as if someone had cut the sun up in pieces and scattered them everywhere. And when the trees turn from etchings into water colors, that is amazing, too. The misty greens and the warm shiny pink buds and the swelling varnished tips on the lilacs. Everything is like a dream.

I am glad to think that this Connecticut land was bought from the Indians legally. There was no bloody struggle such as went on in Deerfield. These Indians wanted the settlers to move in and protect them from the bloody Iroquois. In the old deeds the names of the sachems are listed, signed with their mark. My favorite name is David Hatchet Tousy. One deed is signed by a woman: Muttanumace, her mark. This valley was a garden spot to the Indians, where they came to camp in summer, to fish and raise maize.

When we put in our radishes and lettuce, we always turn up a few arrow-heads — now and then a delicate little quartz bird arrowhead, smooth and beautiful. I like to think of us as part of the long sweep of history, not just separate people dropped down on earth. It's a good, comforting thought that this same earth nourished those dark people, and will nourish us, and those who come after us.

There is an hour of special enchantment after supper these early spring evenings. Light lingers in the sky, what Keats called the "feathery gold of evening." All the cockers and the cats are out in the yard, Clover still after her squirrel and Sister digging for moles. Honey lies dreamily on the terrace; her coat is like the sky and her eyes are very dark. Esmé is pouncing. Then Tigger chases her and they whirl up and down trees in a mad game. If Tigger gets bored, Esmé runs up and slaps him soundly, laying her dark ears back flat.

I may pick up firewood. Or I may just wander around looking at the apple trees against the sky and smelling the spring smell of fresh growing things and cool earth. Spring in New England is not so lush and extravagant as spring in Virginia, but it has its own cool beauty. The green mist of new leaves against the sky, the faint sweet smell of opening lilacs, the sound of the brook singing its silver song. A little later, when it is too dark to see the weeds and stones, the laborers stack their tools by the fence and carry a last pail of water to some special newly set rose or peach tree. Moonlight brims the meadow. A dark feather of wind comes down from the woods.

May

Song for May

Down the dark wood, the silver unicorn
Tramples the fern with hoof of ivory,
But leaves no mark; his delicate, pale horn
Curves silver by the blossoming apple tree.
Silent he moves, nipping the violets
That star the quiet orchard blue and white,
No sound evokes the echo when he lets
His breast sink softly on the slope of night.

Child of old legend, I have known him well,
Who walks May meadows when the moon is
   clear,
Though it be fatal to attest his spell,
The heart finds nothing else on earth as
   dear.

Inconsequential all the truths of day
To one who meets the unicorn in May!

MAY IN NEW England is so close to Heaven that I wonder how the early preachers managed to keep the eyes of their people turned to the future life. Nobody could help being dazzled by the beauty of this world if he rode down a Connecticut country highway in the soft sweet light of a May morning. Heaven enough for me, at any rate; I wish everybody could see it.

The fruit trees have a breathless loveliness. The crab apple tree has starry, snowy blossoms and smells delicious. The bees work there, and a smooth dark catbird sits on the topmost bough. There is the pink apple tree down the meadow. Jill's little sour cherry is a mere corsage compared to the old trees — some Greek goddess should be wearing it.

As if all this weren't enough, the tulips and violets and lilacs are out. The tulips are running out, since we haven't planted new bulbs in a number of years. But the pale gold and white and red and mauve are just as pretty, I think, in the smaller versions. In an old bubble-glass bowl they look lovely.

The primroses have spread, and so have the violets. The primroses are red with bright yellow centers, or pale creamy yellow with gold hearts. The little clusters make the best tiny bouquets; miniature doll pitchers are just right for them, or small antique bottles — which, I suppose, were pill bottles once. My favorite violets are pearl white with blue centers. Massed in a small creamer, they are just as delicate as the primroses are vigorous.

Jill planted a bevy of Johnny-jump-ups and put in pansies. She had considerable help from the spaniels, but managed to save part of the bed by covering it over with wire fencing. Tigger loves to roll in a freshly planted flower bed, and among the vegetables too. Esmé is chasing the first white butterflies of the season.

The white lilacs are the sweetest, but the purple have a thicker cluster. We have two French lilacs; one is a true blue, named President Lincoln, and is wonderfully fragrant.

All through the country you see old lilac clumps:

"A house once stood here, many
   years ago,
   For there are tall old lilacs in a
   row,
   And apple trees that mist the air
   in spring
   With a pink blossoming.
   By a green rosebush, you may
   mark the garden bed.
   These are her memories, that
   passers-by may know
   A house once stood here, many
   years ago."

It must be a fine thing to budget time. The articles about organizing your time always impress me tremendously. They make housework sound as neat as a new slip cover with a zipper. But I never have personally known any women who live by plan. Except possibly the Martins. The Martins lived around the block from us when I was a child, in one of those large, angular Victorian houses so common to little midwestern towns. The kitchen was as big as a tennis court, and gave as much exercise. Getting food to the dining room was practically a safari. Mrs. Martin's sister lived with the Martins. The sisters were slight, vigorous women with an entirely deceptive look of delicacy.

Now the Martin women ran their house by plan. They rose around five-thirty or six and they kept that giant of a house cleaner than a falling snowflake. They also baked and canned and washed and ironed and did church work and attended the literary club. And by eight-thirty or nine in the morning, they could be seen on the wide front porch, sitting side by side in freshly painted Boston rockers. Mamma and I would be dashing by on our way to the grocery store. "I don't see how they do it," Mamma would say, in despair. "They even have the washing on the line!"

I was thinking about the Martin women yesterday. Jill had laid out a full day for Stillmeadow — planting, and painting the kennels, and so on. In a moment of extreme optimism, she made out a schedule for me, too. But when I woke up, the May sun was simply winnowing the air into gold and there was one of those light tender breezes blowing. "I think I'll just run a washing through," I said. "It is so lovely, and you know it might rain on washday."

"I never saw anyone who liked to wash the way you do," said Jill. "Why can't you wait until Monday?"

So I had the tub full in half an hour. Then I had to change the beds, since all the sheets were being washed. I crawled into the linen closet (ours being too low to stand up in) and looked for two pink percale sheets for the bed in the pink room. The shelves were full of sheets, but not matched. I found one pink, one brown, one pale green, and two dark blue ones we had got at a sale. I got out piles of white sheets and laid them on the floor in the adjoining room. I burrowed back in and came out with seventeen unmatched pillow cases.

Forty minutes later, Jill came up to see if I had fainted. I was already far, far behind my schedule. "Oh, my goodness," she said, "whatever are you doing?"

The whole floor was deep with piles of sheets, pillow cases, and bedspreads. I was on the floor, too, madly sorting.

"I'm cleaning the linen closet," I explained with dignity. "Just look in there, it's a shambles."

Jill disappeared, backing in like a crab. I heard thumping sounds. Then she called, "Esmé has been digging holes in the wall, did you know it?" She came out, pulling two old suitcases with her. "I'll have to get the vacuum cleaner," she said, "the wallboard is all over the floor."

After we finished the linen closet, we took a look at the girls' closet. "I think we might make up a box of their clothes and give them away," said Jill. "I don't feel I can bear to see Dorothy go around in those jeans another summer. She can't even sit down in them any more."

Don's closet yielded coils of old rope, which must have been a relic of his cowboy era, a collection of leaky rubbers, a broken tennis racket, a pile of stones, and a stack of funnies.

We had a brief lunch at noon, and then began to sort out the things in my bureau drawers, which led naturally to my doing the table-linen chest in the taproom and Jill sorting the empty boxes in the attic, which we save for mailing everything the children forget when they leave home.

After supper we sat down to rest our aching backs.

"Well," I said, "it's nice we got all the closets and bureaus cleaned. By the way, how did we get started?"

Jill gave me a queer look. "Because you were hunting a pink sheet," she said.

Nothing like this could have happened to the Martin women.

The cockers are busy these days. A large fawn-colored rabbit has lived all winter under the girls' summerhouse. He is a thoughtful rabbit who likes to come out at dusk and go loppety-loppety down the garden rows, eating whatever has poked up through the soft earth. The cockers see him as he emerges from the house, and they fly after him, simply enchanted to be real hunters. There is a flurry of ears, a scrabble of paws, and Melody's high, feminine barking. Silver and Hildegarde sail in like motorized yachts. And after it is all over, Mr. Rabbit slips under the fence and has his evening snack. The cockers feel that they have saved the hearth and home again from the invader, and none of them is at all cast down because they never catch the rabbit.

We have been so much concerned with the problem of happiness these past years. Considering the unthinking happiness of a rabbit chase started me on the subject again. I believe we should let our minds have a little space to meditate. There should be a clear pool in the course at intervals. Just time to think about love and friends and our childhood and all the things that are. And time to realize the wideness of the world and the infinite variety of it.

What is a happy person? And what is happiness? If we never stop to think, how shall we discover what we know? There are many questions we might ask ourselves as we sit in the spring sun for a while and give our minds leisure.

I like what Rupert Brooke wrote to his friend: "I know what things are good: friendship, and work, and conversation. These I shall have." I often think if his life had not been so shortened by the first World War, he would have come to add love to his list of the good.

But he loved life. "The Great Lover" is evidence of his happy passion for the delights of living. "These I have loved

. . . rainbows, and the blue, bitter smoke of wood." And "the little, dulling edge of foam, that browns and dwindles as the wave goes home." This poem is a favorite tonic of mine for what the southerners call "a low-hanging mood."

One thing I have decided about happiness is that it is not something external which you have, or have not. To me it is a quality of the spirit, of being able to realize completely whatever joy you may have and to do this at the moment. Happiness is a thing of now.

This week we had to wash the red and white checked curtains for the two kitchens, and the pale yellow ones for the living room. I was advised to give them "a light starching" to keep them glossy and stiff enough to hang well.

I consulted Jill, doubtfully. "I never did learn how to starch. The boxes," I said, "don't say how much it takes for ten checked curtains."

"Think nothing of it," said Jill, laying down her trowel. "I know all about starch." She came in and thrashed around in the kitchen for some time, finally producing a pan of milky fluid.

We immersed the limp curtains and hung them out. When they were dry, Jill brought them in and sprinkled them, and later still I hooked up the ironer to press them.

"They seem a bit stiff," said Jill, who was watching me.

"Stiff?" I answered, "it's just like running wallboard through the mangle."

I managed to warp them through, with a good deal of effort, and then we hung them. It looked as though the windows were garbed in hoop skirts. The curtains billowed far out into the room, and cut off any outside light. They didn't hang in folds at all, they hung like boards.

The kitchen was suffused with a dim red glow, a murky, faint light. "It reminds me of the little-theater days," I said, "when we used those old red gelatin screens for stage lighting."

I finally lashed down the worst parts with thumbtacks. The kitchen steam will soften them, but the worst of it is, we still don't know how much starch is enough. We know how much is too much.

I hadn't thought of the little-theater days

for some time. We used to have big gangling floods and homemade screens in livid green and fire red and violet. The gelatin stuff always broke in the middle, letting streaks of pure white out. When we wanted moonlight flooding through a lattice window, we turned a seasick green from a flood, and the hero had to be careful not to stand in it, because the effect was ghastly. Usually, as the play approached the climax, somebody would fall over the light cord connecting the floods, and the moonlight would switch off, throwing some confusion on the cast. Or the color screen would slide out of its rusty perch and crash to the floor, and the entire cast would be bathed suddenly in a glare of white.

Our little-theater group was made of sterner stuff, and the fact that nobody ever could be sure what might happen seemed to inspire us with a grim determination to have the play go on.

After the final performance we always had a spread. Some of the best meals I have ever eaten were laid on card tables and benches on the stage, while everyone filled paper plates with thinly sliced ham, chicken salad, golden potato chips, light rolls, steaming coffee leaking through paper cups.

Looking back on it, it seems strange that we hesitated so long over the question of a Siamese kitten. Partly it was because we read such a good cat book first.

"Mercy," said Jill, "cats are delicate! Probably we can't manage to raise Esmé after we get her."

But that was a long time ago. Royal Siamese Queen Merrimac turned out to be a good strong kitten, and an even stronger adult, well able to cope with a dozen cockers, another cat, and the human family she took on. The first week, I remember well, she spoke a great deal of Siamese; in fact, all day and all night she spoke lustily. Nothing made her quiet except being carried in the curve of someone's neck. When we began to understand a little Siamese ourselves, she felt better. But after all, we had never spoken anything but cocker here, and it takes a little time to pick up one of these Oriental languages.

Tigger, the black Manx — what the cat lady called a domestic shorthair — speaks a Connecticut dialect which is quite simple. When he wants to go out, he lies down by the door of his choice and rolls over and over, keeping large glass-green eyes fixed on the nearest person. If he is ignored, he rolls faster. No one can resist it. Then when he wants to get in, he mounts a window sill and utters a firm sentence.

The main difficulty is that his hours are like a night shift at a factory. About ten P.M. he takes his lunch box under one paw and rolls out, and then toward five in the morning he wants his breakfast. He knows where I sleep, and he climbs the window screen nimbly and wails and wails until I admit him. "It's about time," he says firmly. As I sleepily scold him, he rushes at me and purrs like a motorboat. He lifts his funny black face and eyes me blandly with those amazing green eyes. I give in and stagger out for milk.

Tigger is Jill's cat, but Esmé belongs to me. She brought with her a beautiful pedigree full of royal Oriental names, and Jill at once decided that what my cat had, hers should have also. We composed a lovely pedigree for Tigger. We put in Salmon Sam and Broken Jinx,

Sentimental Tom and Catnip Girl, Red Herring and Black Narcissus, back five generations. We wrote it on one of the cocker pedigree blanks, so it is just as impressive as Esmé's.

Esmé has names behind her like Moonglow, Minaret's Tamarind, Siam's Won Lon Son and Imported Champion Siamese Star Prince Favo, which is a mouthful in any language. But perhaps Siam's Sapphire of Khyber is the most romantic name.

The cats have their own ways with food, especially our food. Esmé will rise up suddenly and reach a long arm for a piece of chicken, uttering a fierce demand in Siamese. Tigger sits large and hopeful at one's feet, with an unwinking open gaze. If he is overcome by his desperate state, he makes his voice small and weak and pitiful, as if he might faint at any moment. Then we would be sorry, he says, letting our best cat starve in front of our filled plates.

We used to wander dreamily down the wine-dark streets in the evening, when we were children, carrying our May baskets. They were little colored baskets woven of blue and lemon-yellow straw, and we lined them with soft moss, or fresh green leaves. All day long we had been down along the shining river, gathering sweet purple violets and buttercups, and little nameless pink and white blossoms. Then for special people we hid chocolates or jelly beans under the dewy flowers, and tied ribbon bows on the basket handles.

In twos and threes we went from house to house, slipping up on the porches and setting the baskets inside the screen doors, ringing the bell — oh, exciting and delicious moment — and then running like bunnies to the shrubbery where, giggling and whispering, we peered out to watch the door open and the May basket go in!

The donor of a May basket was supposed to be secret, but there were always ways of knowing, and the one who made the prettiest May basket was stiff with pride for days.

We should preserve this custom, I think, and I hope the children of tomorrow may go out to the sunny meadows and spring woods and gather May flowers for the little reed baskets, and walk singing through the twilight to an early supper and the joy of giving May baskets.

Here in New England, May is planting month, and planting is always a hazardous occupation with us. Melody is so apt to skip through the gate and dig up half a row of something, and Hildegarde wears a mud pack on her beautiful face much of the time. Even the sedate Sister is not above putting a paw in.

I am usually in the kitchen during this period, fixing something more substantial than apples with which to stay the family. Every little while one of the gardeners pokes a head in the door. "Can't you keep those dogs away? How can we get anything done? They're all over everything."

"Well," I say mildly, "you know how they hate to miss anything."

I used not to mind cooking with a bevy of cockers around, and I was fairly adept at stepping from dog to dog, but during the war rationing and shortages made a difference. I couldn't keep buttering toast and passing it around, when there was no butter in the house. Neither could

I slice pieces off a roast, or crisp bacon in the oven for a midday snack, when we hadn't smelled meat for weeks. Then I preferred to have them help in the garden rather than help cook.

Silver and Hildegarde and Melody are certainly unusual cockers. Having been brought up with two cats, they feel they can climb and jump anywhere. We have several wide window sills at Still-meadow, and it is customary for three cockers to be perched on the window sills just where the cats sit too. Melody climbs fences until we are distracted. Keeping her off the road and on our own land is something. And they all three bound up on top of the wellhead to watch the neighbor's dog. Of course, the cover of that wellhead is designed primarily to protect the water, but we fondly hope much mud doesn't sift through the cracks.

Windy and Saxon and Pussy spend their free time digging up the yard after the elusive mole. They are real idealists; they have never caught a mole, but every time I look out the kitchen window I see their up-ended rears and sprays of what might have been lawn flying through the air. The yard is full of regular foxholes, no matter how much we push the roller over it. Be we have decided the happy diggers, red, and black, and gold, are better to look at than smooth turf anyway.

Clover and Snow take a great interest in the new hens that have finally come to live with us. Once or twice the gate has been left open, and nineteen plump hens went skimming in the air like swallows, while the cockers whirled about. Nothing came of it, except the hens were a little hoarse for the rest of the day, from squawking so wildly, and Clover and Snow went around looking as though they had had two on the aisle.

May nights are cool in Connecticut, too cool to eat in the barbecue, unless a fire is burning in the fireplace. The family is firm with me about this. I suggest eating in the barbecue as soon as the ice is off the brook, and I am severely told that barbecue suppers are for warm weather.

I inherit this passion for outdoor eating from my mother. Mother was picnic-minded in a day when it was a little odd to rush off and eat by the roadside except on a regular planned picnic, or a church strawberry festival. Mother liked to pop whatever was handy into a basket and eat in the back yard, or in the front yard, or by the river, or in the lawn swing. And one of my dearest memories is a day when she and I drove together from Pittsfield to Springfield, Massachusetts, and instead of stopping to eat in a restaurant, carried our lunch and ate by the road with the green and dreamy Berkshires behind us and a quick fall of mountain water in the gorge below us. We had sandwiches and deviled eggs and a thermos bottle of coffee, and we talked. The words we spoke are gone down the quick fall of that other stream which is time, but the contentment remains in my memory.

Sometimes I stop to think, now, that every day we are making memories. And I wonder whether I make happy memories enough for my own child. I feel sure that if families would be conscious of the fact that everything they do or say may one day be a memory, there would be less quarreling, fewer harsh words spoken. It is nice to be right, but better to be remembered pleasantly. And there is something so inexorable about the past; you can't change it. You can only try to make today a good one before it, too, slips into the past.

May is almost a perfect month in many ways. One is that now flowers can come into the house. And no matter how involved we may be with the house, the garden, the dogs, there will always be time to arrange flowers. And bouquets will be happy in glass pie plates, wooden mixing bowls, old sugar bowls, bean pots. I have an antique knife box, painted black and stenciled with a colonial design in dull gold. In it go tin cans, cut down to fit. It is lovely with pale misty-gold forsythia and massed jonquils. I use the forsythia for the line of height, and keep the jonquils low, toward the edge of the box. Add to this one Siamese cat, batting the flowers around with a brown velvet glove, and you have something really nice.

The top of an old parlor stove, turned upside down, is good for flowering branches. I like apple blossoms, even though the petals fall so fast. The whole house smells of apple blossoms as long as they last.

Then come the iris, colored like the gold of Ophir or like pale amethyst. We have also a lot of the yellow-brown ones that somehow remind me of small leopards in color. They are the least pretty of the iris, but massed in a copper bowl, they are elegant. Iris doesn't arrange very easily, being spiked and stiff, but if you cut the stems in varying lengths, use some buds and half-open blooms, and mass some dark, full ones at the center and low part of your bouquet, you will be surprised at how graceful the effect will be.

There is much to do in the country in May. The bulk of the planting must be done. Most things are planted when the maples are in bud, or when they are in leaf. I often wonder what those gardeners do, who have no maples to help them chart their course. The only way we get peas at all is to plant them early enough to mature before the aphis arrives. We raise only the edible-podded peas, which are simply delicious and do not have to be shelled. The tender yet crisp pods are wonderful. And all you do to cook them is to break them in one-inch lengths, drop them in a little boiling salted water, and let them cook until the pods are easily pierced by a fork.

Asparagus and rhubarb come in heavily now, and this means the putting-up season is on us again! We freeze both. We used to can them before we had the freezer, but they are better frozen, because they keep their crispness and taste like freshly picked products.

We cut the rhubarb in one-inch lengths, and pack it in round freezer containers, with sugar between the layers. The asparagus we plunge in boiling water for three minutes, then in ice water, then pack it in flat pint or quart containers. The secret of successful freezing is to pick, blanch, and pack as fast as possible, and to seal the container tight. If air gets in, the moisture is drawn out, and freezer burn results.

We also freeze asparagus soup, which we make from the tough ends of the stems. I follow the standard recipe for the soup, but always add a little minced onion for a pickup in flavor.

It is wonderful in January to have fresh rhubarb, and fresh asparagus with drawn butter.

The picket fence must have a new coat. It should be done before the roses are too far along. I thought we might buy a couple of cans of white paint, keep several brushes ready, and ask every guest to do his picket while I fix dinner. I like to paint, but I can't paint pickets. It's the most maddening job in the world; you never seem to be getting anywhere. The line of unpainted pickets stretches to the horizon, and there are no individual differences in the pickets to assure you that you have progressed. If you are painting outside, sixteen spaniel noses are thrust through the pickets, toward you, and rows of wistful dark eyes implore you to let them out. The noses are already frosted with white paint; it's very hard to paint around a sniffing nose that sticks out between two freshly white pickets. If you are painting inside, it is worse. The dogs have to be shut up, and the sound of mourning fills the land.

The May evenings are filled with tender light. After supper everyone dashes outdoors for a last hour. Honey likes to help me dig dandelion greens. I usually sit down with a basket at my side and a sharp knife to cut the plants out. Then Honey rolls over and leans against my neck, kisses my ear, and offers assistance. Her nose is probably already brown with dirt from the tulip bed, and she undoubtedly has been sitting on the violets. If I can persuade her to lie down by the basket, I go on digging. But when Melody and Silver find out where I am, the game is up. Nobody can dig dandelions with two cockers on the back of her neck.

Dandelion greens are a nuisance to get ready, but they are worth it. They are easier to clean if you soak them half an hour in a large pan of cold water, then lift them out and wash them in running water. Give them a final rinse of very hot water. They should be cooked with salt pork or bacon bits in the water, and served with a little butter. Jill likes hers with vinegar. Their bitter rich flavor is one of spring's best treats. And I often think how eagerly our forefathers must have greeted them, after a winter of potatoes, dried squash, and pumpkin and cabbage!

Another month for gardening stoop. The tender vegetables all go in, later the glad bulbs are planted. Suckers are cut from the lilacs. But what a month of glory! The old apple trees on all the country roads and on the green hillsides fill the air with sweetness. Plum and peach and cherry are in blossom. The pear trees are silver fountains.

Lilac time. Now we are repaid for the endless battle with oyster scale as the lilacs lift their amethyst and blue-purple sprays. A single lilac flower is one of the most perfect of God's creations — the little star with its four points and the translucent color and the heavenly scent.

Lilacs are such home-keeping shrubs, too. They keep growing where old houses have vanished, guarding the doorway which is no longer there. When I was a child we used to drive up the Northern Peninsula in Wisconsin in lilac time. Where the old log cabins had been built the dark green lilacs grew, heavy with sweetness.

The old chimney, built of rough stone, would mark the center of the house. Sometimes a tilted lintel stone was there, and now and then a few not-yet-rotted beams. But the lilacs took the sadness from the place.

I like them best in grey stoneware jars or old salt-glazed pitchers. The leaves are so glossy and beautifully shaped I use them all summer for bouquets.

Now we can begin to eat outdoors, and drink in the beauty while we comfort the inner man and woman. This also comforts the inner spaniel. Every mouthful we take is watched from plate to mouth by a row of earnest wistful eyes. The motto of our dogs is, "What's good enough for one is good enough for all."

I keep a soup kettle simmering for the dogs, to help with their feeding. I begin with plenty of onions, cut fine, some chopped garlic, any meat scraps or bones or extra fat or bacon edges, or fowl bones and skin. Then I keep adding whatever I can — outside leaves of chard, lettuce, stem ends of asparagus (not too much of this), clean potato skins, which are loaded with vitamins. Whatever vegetables I am cooking for the family, I spare a little for the dog kettle. Then I thicken the broth before serving with bread crusts, bits of toast, leftover dry cereals, or a handful of rice or barley. This soup, with some dry dog food added, keeps the dogs in fine condition, coats glossy, eyes shining and feet skipping. It's more work than dishing out chopped beef, the way we used to do, but it makes good meals.

Saxon could eat all day long with pleasure. A plummet dropped in his tummy would never strike bottom. Sister is fussy. Snow and Clover are always hungry. Honey acts as if she were doing me a real favor by eating her own meal, but longs for half of mine.

I am sure New England is happy in May. The very softness of the air expresses it, and the whole earth with the sweet spread of flowers and greening fields is happy. Tiny silvery minnows flash in the amber brook, and the birds sing in the apple trees.

Even the cows have a dreamy pleasant look as they wander in the pasture. I wonder if they forget in winter that there is a season of succulent grass and warm sun. Or does a mother cow ever communicate to a winter calf that when he gets older he will be surprised at what will happen?

Now it is warm enough on these May evenings to sit in the back yard while the stars come slowly out in the eternal depth of the sky. The radio is on in the house, and the music comes out through the open door, even sweeter when it is blended with dusk. The cockers settle down on the terrace, paws folded in, and ears limp at last.

The May moon is white as foam. And the May night is sweet as first love. And the heart is lifted up by the happiness which is spring.

When it is too dark to see, there is a feeling of real ecstasy about a hot bath, supper, and a warm spring evening to sit and read in, or listen to the radio, or hear our favorite records. A nice time for the lovely "Im Wunderschönen Monat Mai." Marian Anderson sings it so perfectly in her rich warm voice. Or for early American ballads. Not for Bach or César Franck or the high emotions of hearing Beethoven. Something like Mozart. Or the gay Joseph Marais songs of the South African veld.

Bob dips into a garden article. Jill announces that it was the tenth of May when Ethan Allen took Ticonderoga, in the twilight before dawn. Honey keeps one wary eye out, in case any member of the family feels like looking in the icebox for a snack. Esmé and Tigger, who have done no lick of work all day, suddenly get very busy and open cupboard doors looking for mice.

Bob happily remembers where he found three morels last year, and says he will go again tomorrow for a hunt. Of all the mushrooms in the world, there is none so sweet as a morel. They come in violet time and look like triangular sponges.

The only other wild mushrooms we venture are the fairy rings which grow in circles in the grass, under old apple trees, or in the meadow. They are fine for breakfast with scrambled or shirred eggs. They make wonderful sandwiches, browned in butter with onion, chopped fine, and well salted and peppered.

There are many possibilities for a bedtime snack. The queen of all is, of course, cold fried country chicken. If there is any hamburger for tomorrow's dinner, it will go now, in flat cakes, broiled and laid on toast or a fat bun.

These differ from meal hamburgers in being seasoned more highly and made wafer-thin, and for onion lovers, being further embellished with a paper-thin wedge of sweet onion. Sweet red onion for this. Tomorrow we can eat something else, if the meat is gone. There is something leisurely and sociable about a late snack.

De la Mare makes a last sweetness for the day. Under the May moon, the cockers are dreaming in their beds, the cats are walking quiet in the dew, the family is ready to turn out the lights. As I poke my head out to say farewell to the day I think aloud:

"I met at eve the Prince of Sleep,
His was a still and lovely face,
He wandered through a valley steep,
Lovely in a lonely place."

The white light of the moon falls on the blossoming fruit trees, on the sleeping meadows, on the far dark of the hills. All's well at Stillmeadow in the lovely May night.

When I am wakeful, I like to listen to the stillness of the hours after midnight.

The very wings of peace fold over our valley. I can feel how good the world is, and how unnatural it is for mankind to be so ridden with fear and hate. We are all born into the same world, we breathe the same air, that miraculous envelope wrapped round our small planet, we are nourished on the same fare of food and water, and we are one in death at the end.

Seeing this is so, we are communally bound together. We are brothers, whether we like it or not! And every time we invent a nice new buzz bomb or jet rocket, it is our own whom we prepare to destroy.

The moon is wiser, for she sheds equal light over the hills of Judea and the silvered meadows outside my New England window.

June

Song for June

Summer is not the golden blaze of sun,
Nor lilac dark along the country lane,
Nor opal morning where the cool brooks
    run,
Nor velvet midnight laced with sudden rain.
Neither is summer the unfolding rose,
The frosty blue of berries ripening,
Nor tawny silken tassels down the rows
Where the tall corn makes dusty
    whispering.

These are but part of summer, not her
    heart,
Not the deep marrow that sustains the
    bone,
Investiture, yet from the whole apart,
For more than these is summer's self alone.

Summer is in your eyes that look on me
With sweet fulfillment of spring ecstasy.

IT MIGHT SEEM as if June were an old story, with so much poetry written about it, and so many songs sung. And yet every time it comes it is as much of a wonder, as much of a delight.

If I had Aladdin's lamp and the usual three wishes, the first would always be, "Give me the first day of June." The whole, complete day, with the sky-blue dawn, and the golden noon, and the violet dusk, and the silvered night. With early roses unfolding and a hummingbird over the border. And a whole packet of smells too. New-cut grass, and pea vines, and freshly hoed garden soil.

When I was growing up, June meant the end of school, and going away for the summer to the cottage. Such packing and unpacking and buying of groceries! And when the car was loaded, there was room for everything except me and one large Irish setter. Papa and Mamma were in front, the lunch basket under Mamma's feet. We always started off with a flourish and got as far as Kaukauna before we remembered something had been left behind. Then we drove back madly and retrieved it and started all over again.

Nothing was more wonderful than the first sight of the cottage. Pine needles had drifted over the steps. The water was that deep June blue, which always made me wonder why they called it Green Bay. Timmie would leap from the car and frantically begin on the squirrels. We would go into the cottage and the smell of winter was still there, and the good odor of unpainted pine boards. There was never any dust. Mamma could whisk the newspapers from the kerosene stove and have a hot supper in no time. I always flew into my heavy wool bathing suit and rushed to the shore. The icy water was delicious. It was almost like being born again.

Now in New England, June brings many activities. The late planting must be done, and Jill is forever in the garden, bent in a permanent curve. The rabbits are there, too, at dusk. Somehow, no matter what damage they do, I cannot work up any resentment against rabbits. They are so soft and their eyes have a melting wistfulness. I like their loping gait too.

The pest that causes us the most trouble is the mole. Not only the ridges he raises in the lawn are bad, but the digging the cockers do makes it worse. Once the moles ate up a whole tulip bed which we expected would be especially beautiful, since all the bulbs were pedigreed.

There are many remedies for moles, but none of them has been very successful for us. Pouring old crankcase oil in the runs is a good one, provided the dogs do not dig in the same spot and get a good oiling of muzzles and ears.

June is one of the easiest months as far as menus go. With the first fresh garden crops, meals can be simple and quick. And oh, that first salad of baby lettuce leaves just uncurling, crisp red radishes, young chard, sweet scallions! I use a plain French dressing with a clove of garlic steeped in it.

Broilers are for Sunday, and Fay Clark's baked broilers are elegant. She piles cooked rice or well-seasoned poultry dressing in a baking pan and lays the broilers on top, seasoning them rather highly, then bakes them in a moderate oven (350°) until the broilers are tender. When any chicken is done, a sharp fork will pierce to the bone easily. It is hard to see why so often you get underdone fried chicken, for when you test with a fork, if it is not done, red juice will ooze out after the fork.

Deep-dish rhubarb pie or rhubarb cobbler is my choice for June dessert until strawberries are ripe. Of course strawberry shortcake, made correctly, is the dessert above all comparison. A rich biscuit dough is what it takes, and no sponge or cake mixture. And the berries must be partly crushed, sweetened and set in a bowl near the stove so they will be slightly warm. This brings out the sweet rich flavor. The biscuit dough should be baked in round tins, split and buttered, then simply deluged with berries. Topped with a mound of fluffy whipped cream.

The best way to serve shortcake is to make it a whole meal. And eat all you can hold. We like it for supper, and if the day is fine, we can eat out under the apple trees. Honey especially loves whipped cream and the last bits of the sweet biscuit on the platter.

June in New England is like a lover's dream made tangible. Color and scent and sound; the hills indeed sing. Dawn comes so fresh and cool, and dusk flows like a still river into the deep sea of night. Noons are tranquil gold. There is nothing stern or sober about our Northern countryside now; even the grey rock ledges are gently blurred with silvery green lichens, and in the great cracks time has chipped out, a thousand tiny plants get a precarious hold.

Lilacs make their own purple dusk all day, or lift dreamy clusters of pure pearl. Their scent is cool and mysterious. It is surely one of the most romantic smells — it reminds me of old deserted gardens where long-vanished ladies come again to walk in the moonlight.

The white lilacs have a special delicacy, a purity. I always feel too solid when I pick them, and pick them I must! Their odor is even sweeter. I am sure in the dark of the moon my unicorn comes on delicate little hoofs to find the place where the white lilacs grow and crop the flowers. I can tell where he has moved, because the leaves are a little swayed aside. His horn is silver and his eyes are amber. A white unicorn feeding on white lilacs would be a fine sight to see.

Briefly, in June, the children drift back to touch home base again for a time. The girls come with fanfare, laden with dirty laundry enough for the armed forces, with runover shoes and broken glasses and cavities in their teeth. With boxes of books tied up with old rope, and with phonograph records in suitcases. The preliminary approach is made by tons of airmail and ordinary mail and postcards. As they get closer the phone begins to ring. None of their friends, it appears, has any idea when they will arrive, how long they will stay, or where they are going when they are mended and repaired and ready for combat again in the mysterious outside worlds parents wot not of.

The culinary department has been stocked for some days with everything that can be baked, boiled, roasted, or whipped up in advance. It appears that no food of any kind has passed the lips of the younger members of our family for weeks. In a semi-fainting condition, they fall into the kitchen and admit they are at the point of collapse.

I wonder whether it was simpler when the children were still at home, and June brought the last events of the school year right on our own doorstep. Pageants and plays, Sunday school projects. The children making the last ash trays, and giving concerts on primitive instruments. There is something very odd to me in a pageant. The sight of a small boy in brown cambric, wearing his mamma's fur around his head does not actually suggest Daniel Boone to me; and when he hacks with a cardboard hatchet at a paper mountain, I distinctly do not experience the thrill of the Dark and Bloody Ground. The vision of Cicely as part of a bread line, chanting, "I haven't got a job; I haven't got a nickel," had a shade more reality, as I knew she probably hadn't got a nickel.

Then there was the time when Don had to give a speech in final assembly. I asked him about it, and he said, rather diffidently, "Well, it begins, 'I am an

Athenian citizen.' "

Jill said, "Do you want a sheet or something for a costume?"

"Oh, no," he said, "we're going to wear our regular clothes. I just want my good pants."

The morning of the speech he got up at dawn, and voluntarily washed his face and hands. With his cowlick sopped down and his fringe brushed back, he was ready to mount the rostrum and declaim, "I am an Athenian citizen."

Afterward I asked him how it went. He gave me a solemn look and twisted his feet around the chair legs. "Oh, I gummed the whole program," he said.

I didn't press him. I suppose he forgot just what he was doing as an Athenian citizen, but he preferred to let the tale be untold.

Then there was always the school year book. I remember the day I found Cicely absorbed in Bartlett's Quotations, looking for suitable verses to be printed under the senior pictures.

"I found one that just fits Mary," she said doubtfully. "You know Mary is so dumb. 'Be good, sweet maid, and let who can be clever.' Do you think that would get by?"

"No, I don't," I said.

"Then we found a lovely one about a quiet mind is richer than gold," she went on, "but we couldn't think of anybody at Bradley with a quiet mind. It's really very difficult."

"We always used 'Queen rose of the rosebud garden of girls,'" I said reminiscently, "and 'Her voice was ever soft, gentle, and low, an excellent thing in woman.' We used that for someone we just couldn't fit to anything else."

Cicely sighed, "I've got to be in a play, too, and I'm tired of being abstract Truth and Wisdom. I wish just for once I could be a regular character."

Pageants, plays, parties. Oh, yes, parties. And Dorothy's first evening dress for the Junior Prom. That time it looked as though Jill would have a nervous breakdown as an after effect. Unless you know how fourteen-year-olds are, you would think that a city the modest size of New York might have an evening dress or two for a high school dance. But it turned out to be more impossible to find a dress that Dorothy would wear than to pile Pelion on Ossa.

The question of the evening coat was worse. One solitary evening coat was at last found and delivered, and turned out to be a size too small.

"You'll have to wear your sport coat," said Jill.

"I won't," said Dorothy desperately. "I can't!"

"Then you'll have to borrow Miss Brown's white wrap."

"No, I can't wear that, either." Dorothy was determined. "I just won't wear anything."

"You will too," said Jill. "It's too cold to racket around in a sleeveless wisp of silk."

Meanwhile the problem of getting Dorothy to a beauty parlor for a little renovation was engaging both Jill and me. At that age Dorothy was allergic to any form of hair care. By the time Dorothy was groomed, gowned and off to the dance, we had both earned a stay in a sanitarium.

Then there were our early struggles with their music lessons. Dorothy had been taking piano lessons for about two years, rather idly, but at least taking them, when Jill decided it was time for

Don to "take" something too. Tooting penny whistles and bursting paper bags under our noses had gone on long enough, she felt. So she told him she was getting him a trombone for his birthday.

"I don't want any old trombone," said Don firmly. "I won't look at it."

Jill described the joys of a trombone. Don burst into tears and retired. For about a week life consisted of hysterics, violent scenes, bouts of tears over the trombone. But Don always rejected anything new, so Jill persisted. On his birthday he unwrapped all his presents and was very happy. Then he said, suspiciously, "Is this all? Every single thing?"

"Well, no," said Jill. "The trombone will be out tomorrow."

She dragged him down for his first lesson at the music factory in New York. The next time I saw him, Don came bounding at me with this large shining thing.

"Listen here," he said. "Listen here!" He shot his arm out and a loud blast from the trombone nearly blew my head off. "It's my new trombone," he said proudly. "The man says I can prob'ly be a great artist — a great one — like

Tommy Dorsey! I got a natural lip!"

And a few weeks later Jill had to turn in his beginner's trombone for a bigger and better instrument at a much higher price.

Shortly afterward Jill met some prominent musician at a dinner and was discoursing on Don and his trombone, as a mother will do.

"But why did you pick a trombone?" he asked. "A trombone is always played by guess and by golly. It's all in how far you slide your arm out. And did you hear the Philharmonic Sunday? In the trombone solo the fellow never hit the right pitch one time! What did you pick a trombone for?"

Jill blushed faintly. "Well, I always wanted to play a trombone myself," she said.

A few days after that I bought Cicely a guitar. Not long before we had heard a man play the guitar and sing folk songs. He had spent fifteen years doing research on folk music, and sang early English, Creole, cowboy, and Negro songs, many of them never in print. Cicely and I had talked until almost one o'clock that night about "Green Grow the Rushes, O,"

"The Streets of Laredo" and "The Glory Trail."

"But how in the world did you come to pick out the guitar for her?" a friend asked me.

I blushed faintly. "Well, I always wanted to play the guitar myself," I said.

This morning I ate breakfast with as good company as I wish to see. Honey sat by my side, beautiful and golden. Next to her sat Tigger, blacker than ebony. On the table perched Esmé with her smoky Siamese coloring and her blue, blue eyes. Star stood on the other side with Pussy beside her. A good recipe for a human reducing breakfast is a lot of good things to eat, and three spaniels and two cats to eat with.

When I get to Heaven, I am not going to put on golden shoes or cast down golden crowns around a glassy sea or play on my harp. No, I am going to eat all the hot bread and potatoes I want. Cinnamon rolls, pinwheel biscuits, nut muffins, French-fried potatoes, baked potatoes, creamy mashed potatoes. Potato fluff. Butter will go well, too. And fresh-made jam. Or clear amber honey.

For anyone known as "a born cook," reducing approaches anguish. It is no laughing matter to skip lightly into the kitchen and fix barbecued spareribs, juicy and rich and spicy and abounding in calories, and watch the family smack their lips over the platter while you eat a lonely lamb chop — broiled, fat cut off, fat being the best part — and a dish of shredded cabbage garnished sweetly with a slice of lemon.

But I like the fresh green vegetables too. The first thinning of beets and onions steamed in butter is also a dish that might go on any heavenly menu. Dandelion greens are delicious, the faint bitter taste makes them excellent with meat; and when we get them from our lawn we are doubly satisfied, for it is actually killing two birds with one stone. It helps the lawn and feeds us.

The queen of all greens is turnip salad as it is cooked in Virginia. On my last visit there, a friend was giving a luncheon for me and she said, "Can you suggest the menu?"

"Yes," I said, "turnip greens and cornbread."

I ate four helpings of the greens, including the delicious lumps of salt pork which were cooked with them. And when I saw a platter of baked silver-gold onions, my cup was full — and so was my stomach. I'll never forget that meal, and I expect they are still talking about the amount of greens one person could consume.

It was on this occasion that I learned how to cook turnip greens for I sadly said, "They don't taste right in the North."

"Yankees can't cook them," she laughed.

"Tell me."

She called in her cook, Sally. "You just cooks 'em in a ir-run pot."

"How long?"

"'Twell they's done."

After twenty minutes I gathered something. Real turnip greens take several hours to cook! I had cooked them like spinach or beet tops. But they must simmer on the back of the stove with plenty of salt pork in them for "'round two, three hours." Unlike most greens, they have a peculiarly resistant stem, tough and bitter. Properly simmered, they are melting good.

From now on the house will be full of flowers. I like the Victorian bouquet done in the base of an old oil lamp that has lost its chimney. My friend Ruth Kistner taught me how to fill the bowl of the lamp with water to which a tablespoonful of milk and a teasponful of dye have been added. Any of the package dyes is good. The milk makes the liquid opaque, and the trick is to use a dye which is the same color as the main color of your flowers, or a little darker. It must, however, harmonize with it.

I make the bouquet with the darker, heavier flowers at the base, and the lighter ones at the top. And for all bouquets, I make the height satisfying by measuring the height of the lamp, doubling that measurement, and having the tip of the flowers equal it. Twice the height of the container makes your whole creation artistic.

An all-white bouquet is lovely. So is an all-white garden. Last year at the National Flower Show in New York there was a white garden and it seemed perfect. There were tall pearly white tulips, and white massed shrubs — azaleas, I thought — behind them, and white blossoming fruit trees making a background. There were white pansies for ground cover under the tulips, and the little inner, secret resting place was a frosty white iron Victorian bench. It seemed as if anyone who sat on the wrought-iron bench under the blossoming pear tree might find all her young dreams again.

I learned something about white gardens. There should be one place where a soft color is used, to emphasize the beauty of the white. One shell-pink azalea had been placed in one corner of this garden, and it was echoed in some smaller pink blossoming shrub at the opposite end.

Anyone can make a garden in such a small space that I think all women should have them unless they live in a city apartment. The merest scrap of back yard can make a place of loveliness. I know nothing at all about expert gardening, but I noticed at the flower show that the little gardens all had one central focus, a tiny pool, or a small arbor, or a comfortable place to sit. The lines of planting always led to this center of interest. All the gardens at the show were enclosed, too, by higher shrubs, or low trees.

Of course, if we had that white garden, it would have to be up the hill, outside the fence, and far removed from roving cocker paws. And if we made it far away, when would we get time to sit there and dream? And what would the dogs do, when we shut the gate on them? Their sad songs would penetrate even the stillest and whitest of gardens.

I am glad to get the picnic things out again. There are just two necessities in picnic equipment — lightness and a full quota of forks. It is hard to have a crock of hot baked beans, for instance, and then find the forks are ten miles away. I don't like to drink baked beans out of a cup, or to spear them with twigs. I packed supper last night in the light wicker hamper. I keep forks, knives, spoons, salt and pepper and sugar, enameled plates and cups, a can opener, a big knife and paper napkins as standard equipment. I use small covered refrigerator boxes for relishes and small salads. Larger ones are perfect for meat loaves or larger salads, and they weigh very little.

We ate on a warm grey ledge over Eight Mile Brook. The beans were piping hot, the crock wrapped in newspapers and covered with a bath towel. Brown bread sandwiches went with the beans, and there were radishes and scallions. Hot coffee, hot cocoa, and fresh thin sugar cookies finished the picnic.

We watched the sun go down along the curve of the stream. The world was filled with cool green light and the water shone like pewter. Down the road came a herd of Holsteins, slow and contented, and a boy and a dog came with them. The boy whistled, the dog wagged his tail.

Don came up to eat the last four cookies, and as Cicely and Dorothy were out of sight, he got them.

"When are you going to make doughnuts?" he asked, munching happily. The girls came up with handfuls of sweet wild strawberries. Jill, of course, was trying to take a picture of the sunset. If it were good, I reflected idly, it would appear in some salon as Full Moon on the River, or as Dawn in the Country. Pictures seem to work out that way.

There is a special softness to these late spring evenings in Connecticut. Light lingers on the water long after the hills and fields are deep in dusk. The air has a cool deep sweetness, and is not a single scent but a thousand mingled odors. You can smell, too, the evening water.

Putting the hamper back in the car, I saw above the young maples the first star, round and clear. And into my mind came the words of the psalm: "My cup runneth over."

Just then Cicely loped into sight. "Mamma! A snake! Here's a snake!"

And I thought, "Even in Eden!"

This is the time of roses and puppies in the sun. It's the best time in the year to have young puppies coming along. They blossom along with the roses, and the sun is not yet too hot, the ground is not damp, the temperature is fairly even. They can scramble over the lawn, and what a lovely-smelling world they find with their soft, eight-week-old noses. I always think late spring is a good time for people to begin with a puppy, if they aren't used to raising them.

Yesterday we washed a whole litter and the mamma. I have heard perfectly good authorities say that puppies should never be washed. I don't believe it. There was a time when good authorities said children shouldn't be washed in winter. There were families who sewed themselves up in long underwear every fall, and how they lived through until spring I can't see.

A puppy never should be chilled or left wet. I use a good warm thick suds and have warm bath towels ready. A sponge is necessary, a soft, old-fashioned sponge. I dip the baby in the suds, sponge him well, being careful to get the ears clean, but not full of water. Then I rinse in clear warm water and rub him thoroughly dry with towels, discarding them as fast as they get damp. When the fur is dry and fluffy, the baby gets a warm meal.

We don't have much trouble with fleas, and I had a fine illustration of why, recently. The puppies and the mother had picked up some very active ones from an outside source. I couldn't find our regular flea-killing soap, but Jill discovered some very expensive dog soap which had been given to us, and we used that. But after the babies were all fluffed out, several small paws began to scratch again, and we found the fleas were in excellent shape. We got out a dog spray and gave them a thorough treatment with that.

And still the fleas were there. In desperation Jill began a new search for the tried and true flea-killing soap, and finally found it. We began over again. The fleas dropped in the water like rain. On the towels the last fleas flopped out, cold and stiff. This flea killer is not rinsed away, but is allowed to remain in the coat, and will protect the puppy for three weeks. We have used it a long time, but this is the first time we have had a chance to compare its virtues with those of other products. There are, of course, a number of good flea powders and dog soaps, and DDT may revolutionize the life of the dog, but the instantaneous and complete job done by this kind is its own recommendation.

I used to think of the whippoorwill as a most romantic bird; once or twice I heard one crying in the north woods in

Wisconsin and the sound was exquisite. But that was before I got so intimate with the whippoorwill. He has lost his charms for me. All night long I am jerked from my sleep at ten minute intervals, not by one lone one, but by all his sisters and his cousins and his aunts. I never knew they came in bevies, but if this is just one family group going on so furiously, I know they have sore throats.

The voice of the whippoorwill has a penetrating quality, a kind of feverish intensity as he implores me to whip poor Will. I rise up and assure him, and his relations, just as feverishly, that I would be glad to if I could only get my hands on them. Romance or not, I like a few hours' sleep.

We drove over to call on a friend last night, a friend made on account of Esmé. Mr. Bellamy has a pair of Siamese cats, extremely regal and practically brought up on show ribbons. So he came to inspect Esmé, and we went to inspect his two, and there we were. That is the nicest thing about an interest; it always involves making some nice new friend who has the same interest.

Mr. Bellamy lives alone in the most

charming house anywhere in these hills, except maybe Stillmeadow. His house is not old, but he collected old material for it over a period of two years and then designed it in the authentic style. Even after he assured us he had built it, we couldn't believe it wasn't built in 1700. Old batten doors, pine paneling, wide old floor boards, old hardware, small-paned windows, old cupboards; and then old furniture, really old — just the kind of a house to dream about. It is built just above a roaring, rushing trout stream, and the sound of rushing water comes sweet and cool in the bedroom windows.

Nearly every room has a fireplace or an old, old stove, shapes and sizes I have never seen outside a museum. The living room has a Franklin that fits in the corner — a three-cornered stove, as it were — and over it hangs a collection of old wrought-iron treasures, such as iron stands, the kind old irons were rested on while Mother laid the bombazine on the ironing board.

Then he has bottles, old twisted glass bottles, and one which was once clear glass, which time has changed to pale hyacinth purple. He found it in a dump, and it is as lovely as a piece of ancient Egyptian glass.

Besides all this bounty, he has sixteen sheep. I know sheep are very hard work, like any livestock. But the sound of sheep bells in the twilight, mingled with the sound of that trout brook took me instantly to magic casements opening on the foam of faery lands forlorn. And a phoebe had built a nest, lined with sheep wool, in the wellhead!

"Oh, it is so lovely and peaceful here," I said.

Mr. Bellamy gave me an odd look. "You have any whippoorwills over at Stillmeadow?" he asked.

Whippoorwills!

I read a magazine article yesterday about the delights of painting lawn furniture. I hate to disagree with the printed word, but I can hardly picture the man, woman or child who would laugh with joy at the prospect of painting a dozen lawn chairs. And having just put the third coat on our own, I would just like to hold a brief conversation with the author of that article.

Adirondack chairs you can paint on

forever. Slat upon slat, arm after arm. Canvas deck chairs have very little canvas compared to the dozens of rungs, side pieces, feet, back supports. Wicker — only a word about wicker. You don't paint it, you scrouge the brush into every inch. Then after you finally get through and you go in to get the paint out of your hair, it starts to rain.

At least this is the way it works out for me. Lawn furniture should be white, with brightly colored canvas in any shade you like. We have tried every color except black in the annual paint jobs on the lawn furniture at Stillmeadow, and now know that white is the most satisfying. On a smooth — well, nearly smooth — lawn, white furniture looks cool and inviting, and never tires the eye.

But it is fun, when the chairs do get dry, to eat supper at sunset time under the apple trees. We carry out the little charcoal grill and do hamburgers and loll back in immaculate white chairs, resting our coffee on shining white tables. It is all very gay and sweet then, and I forget the dreary job.

This is a kindly village. The post office

is in the general store, and Miss Evangeline and her helpers work in front, behind the store window. They are so pleasant they make handling the mail a gracious thing. They are so pleased when you get the letter you wanted so much from your child. They are regretful if, "No, there's nothing for you today." And they sell me stamps without making me feel inferior. In the city, I dread going to the post office. I approach the stamp window timidly and feel as if I had no right, really, to bother them. And when the fearful fact emerges that I cannot think quickly how many stamps I should get for a dollar, I am withered by a blast of scorn. Mailing a package in the city is a fearful ordeal. But how different it is in the store post office. Miss Evangeline may stop to say she has been picking wild strawberries. In the canning season, everyone within hearing discusses what is being put up.

There are two grocery stores in our village, one garage, and two lumber companies. There is a railroad station, but no trains. Only an occasional freight car of feed or coal comes in. The express comes by truck, and when a package arrives, the agent loads it in your car for you or if it is too big for the car, will help take it to pieces so you can transport it. In the second store you buy meat, if there is any. And Jimmy, who can dress up a turkey to look like a magazine photograph for Thanksgiving, is always ready to chop up a little extra meat for the dogs.

The vegetable man keeps the baskets of fresh vegetables clean and attractive; he picks out the best vegetables carefully, and is as cheerful when you buy one lemon as when you buy an armload.

The garage man put air in the tires just as pleasantly during the war as when gas and oil flowed like the Housatonic. Mr. St. Pierre, who owns the garage and one store, has a slim Doberman pinscher puppy. Usually, when you drive up, Mr. St. Pierre is standing in the door looking anxiously after the Doberman, just to be sure he is all right.

All this adds up to something very important. The war tended to make everyone irritable, nervous, jumpy, and unpleasant. I have a friend who says, "I've been insulted steadily ever since the war started, and it still goes on." Harassed, overtired people all over the country are taking it out on one another. But the people around here just never succumbed to it. And it renews my faith in America all over again because they have stayed kind and patient and pleasant.

It adds up to something else. Life is not, after all, made up of grand moments, grand gestures, glorious achievements. Life is made up of many days filled with small things. Shopping, going to the post office, using the telephone, keeping house — these make up the chief sum of our days. And to me, it seems infinitely greater to make all the people one sees feel a little happier for it than to paint a masterpiece or be in bright lights on Broadway. After we are all gone down the river of time, the simple kindness of those who fulfill their daily tasks graciously will overbalance any special feat.

I believe with all my heart that there are people in all the lands who have this gift of living. There are people with love enough to give their neighbors, whose bounty is like Juliet's — the more they give, the more they have, for both are infinite. And such people must make our new world.

I have moments when I am frightened, as one must be, reading about intolerance and hate that sucks men down in a swampy muck. When the names of loyal Japanese were struck from a roll in the West, when a White worker strikes because a Negro worker has come in, when anti-Semitism raises a cobra hood. There are plenty of such things to sicken the heart, and it is only realistic to face them.

But then I count the other people, the friendly folk, and I am comforted, and I have hope.

I believe fundamentally the war was fought to preserve the individual, and somehow, in spite of mistakes and political chicanery, and the weakness of men's judgment, I believe it has. I believe in the end, a man will be able to walk freely on the earth, and hold his head high, just because he is a man.

When I watch the June dusk, and see the sky glow with the color of moonstone, and hear a farm wagon creaking down the shadowy road, I know how beautiful the world is.

Surely Gibran was right, and sadness is a wall between two gardens.

July

Song for July

Many a man has lived on dreams alone,
Nourished his heart on what he never had,
Many a woman makes her bread from
    stone,
And dreaming brims the cup of many a lad.
Mariners steer tall ships against the moon
With never a port in sight, but hope of one,
And oftentime the passionate bud of June
Withers untimely in too hot a sun.

This we know well, and yet we raise our
    eyes
On summer evenings when all wings are
    still
And there again behold familiar skies,
Silvered with stars above the darkest hill.

We see the stars, and easily may mark
How swift their glow diminishes the dark.

I LOVE TO look at the pictures of summer lounging that fill the magazines. Women in frosty white play suits and alpargatas (romantic word, that is), men in cool elegant summer slacks and pastel shirts (Cicely used to call them up-tops, when she was little). And oh, the chaise longues or beach chairs, the little wicker tables laden with tall glasses and mint-cool drinks. There is such an air of leisure as they sun-bathe and acquire that lovely magazine tan. Often a stately gentleman great Dane or a lady Dalmation in her black-and-white summer print sits motionless just at the edge of the picture.

Stillmeadow summer lounging never remotely resembles this. On a hot July afternoon I may decide to take a sun bath in the back yard. The summer play suits are always faded and have paint spots on them. Instead of alpargatas I don white moccasins, well-carved with toothmarks

271

from puppies' chewing. My hair, alas and alack, is never freshly waved for the moment, but is what the family refers to as my summer bush. I take up my book, which always turns out to be something much too massive to hold while lounging — something like Beard's *Rise of American Civilization* or *Thomas Jefferson*.

I tiptoe to the yard so I won't get interrupted, and ease myself into the chaise longue. This object may have its dreams of bygone glory, but now it needs paint on the white metal frame (not frosty any more). The pad has quite a lot of holes in it. Silver has never outgrown her puppy days, and Melody isn't above a passing chew on anything so nice and soft to the teeth.

I look up at the sky and see the lovely clear blue and I close my eyes to feel the golden sun on my lips. Then plunk! plunk! plunk! Three cockers land on me, amidships. They have discovered me. Oh, how marvelous, how exciting, how very gay! The book falls on the grass and Hildegarde sets a damp paw on the open page. Four more cockers emerge joyfully from the house and join the party. Of course, I have been around the place all day long, but this is different. This is summer lounging. The table goes over, and Melody puts a tentative tongue in the glass to see if lemonade is really all right for a girl to drink. It's too sour.

When I can breathe again, I notice two cats have materialized, looking very photogenic. Silver makes a slight gesture toward Esmé and gets slapped. I try to explain that all ten cockers can't lie on the same chaise longue with me. The phone rings with peculiar urgency in the house, and the hour is over.

Some people might think the cockers could be shut up. Well, I have tried that. I found, however, that lounging in plain view of the kennel fence did not make me feel elegant or relaxed or peaceful at all. The mourning faces pressed wistfully against the wire, the hopeful tails twiddling every few moments, the whoofing noises as I turned a page, not to mention Melody's frantic efforts to climb out — these might be withstood by a really sane woman; but for me, I always weaken and get up and go over to let them join me. There is something about that passionate desire cockers have just for your wonderful presence close to them — it is something that makes you humble and grateful just to experience.

The garden vegetables are a source of endless satisfaction to me now. I think many people who began to garden because of the war will never be without a garden again. It seems to me our whole national way of life has changed. Even dyed-in-the-wool city dwellers will like to go weekends to a little house in the hills, work in the sun in the day and stretch their muddy shoes in front of a fire, while their own home-cured bacon sizzles in the pan.

To have a small country place requires determination and faith in the future, and a cash income, small or large. You can't make a fabulous fortune raising things, whether it be mushrooms or muskrats. But you can live better on less, and you can save more. You need cash for the light bills or kerosene, for the coal or wood, for clothes and medical bills.

Of course, if you buy an old house, you must be very strong-minded, or it will eat up all the money you have as fast as you get it. An old house demands. It is so beautiful and you love it so, surely you can spare some more money to do over the cellar, or insulate, or get new storm doors. You may dream of living in it as it is, camping out, but just move in and you will be bending every effort to satisfy the little darling.

How often have friends of ours bought little old houses and said, nose in air, "It is merely a place for relaxation for us. We don't want to work at it."

I visit them a few months later. It's one of my favorite sports. They are always clad in old clothes, and greet me as though they loved me but really could hardly stop painting the kitchen floor or sawing up the boards for the shelves John is going to build "all by himself!" Then you do a tour. Here is where the barbecue will go as soon as they get a minute to build it. And they must scrape the paneling in the front room, and they plan to wax it themselves winter weekends, and also paint the bedrooms upstairs.

The yard, where they planned to lie at ease and read books, is already chewed up by amateur attempts to dig and plant. They hardly have time to eat anymore, they say, and they look tired out but oh, so radiant. I never, never say dreamily, "I thought you weren't going to do anything to your place." I offer them violets and iris from our beds. They will collect them as soon as they get that closet under the stairs built.

The air is sweet with fragrance in July; warm grasses, summer flowers, ripening beans and golden-tipped dill. The herbs are spreading; how silver-gray the sage grows, how blue the borage flower. The weeds in the garden begin to have their way, after the first week in July. There is a new school of thought, as a matter of wonder, that believes in weeds! Their shade keeps moisture in the soil, they say.

Time to pick the ripe vegetables, time to can, preserve, and freeze. Those first tender green string beans must be gathered at just the right moment before they begin to harden their pods in maturity. The first baby beets are the ones to put down in jars, either pickled or plain, and of course our old friend, the chard, is doing its stuff all too faithfully. When it gets ahead of us, Jill cuts the biggest leaves and gives them to the chickens for a special treat.

Rose Wilder Lane has the best device for storing jars that I ever saw. She takes old bricks and supports her shelves with them. She can thus raise or lower a shelf by adding or subtracting a brick. The shelves may be taken down for cleaning. And it looks so neat and tailored.

The moonlight is whiter than pearl over the meadow these July nights. The small businesses of the day and the worries are magicked away by the soft glow. You can step from the door of the little white house into a white foam of moonlight on the dark crest of the wave of night.

Esmé steps delicately, on her cinnamon velvet feet, along the terrace where the dew has not fallen. Her eyes are lit with moonlight; they are sapphire flame. On the fence, black Tigger sits, his body melting in night, but his eyes shining, too, pure topaz or sea green as the light reflects in them.

This past year I have been making strenuous efforts to learn Spanish. I have read so many articles about keeping up with the children's interests, and Cicely and

Spanish are practically synonymous. And when I realized that she was about to receive her Master's degree in Linguistics, whereas I still could speak only English, I felt I should take steps!

Possibly I would have let it go, under the pressure of everything else I had to do, but the last time we were in the city I attempted to get a radio repaired in the neighborhood shop, which turned out to be run by an Argentinian. I told him the radio would not work. He responded with a long statement in Spanish, with what seemed to be a question at the end. I told him again that I simply wanted it fixed. "It will not run," I said, speaking slowly and firmly. He placed his hand over his brow, fixed me with anguished eyes and delivered some kind of oration. Then we went into pantomime. We waved our arms, pointed, wrung our hands, raised our voices, with much working of the lips.

Finally I rushed to the phone and called Cicely. "Come quick," I said, "neither of us can speak either language!"

Cicely came, and burst into voluble Spanish. The look of relief, of gratitude, that spread over the man's face was pathetic. They discussed the state of the radio, its diagnosis, settled everything, while I stood dumbly by the counter. Finally the man began pointing at me and shaking his head. *Mamacita,* he was saying, was very stupid. Cicely was obviously Spanish, but how did she explain such a *mamacita?* Perhaps the papa?

No, Cicely said, she had learned it at school. *Es imposible,* he opined. Then he told her the story of his life, his being in the army, his adventures in getting to the United States; and by the time we left, he followed us to the door, saying, "May God follow your footsteps." He had found one sane American, that was evident.

Shattered by this experience, I began to study Spanish. I may say the struggle has been epic. After some months, I now have reached the stage of being able to hold a conversation in the language, provided that it is confined to the subject matter of my textbook. Radios and radio tubes are far from my ken, but I can say that the General Gomez is going to the war, but the king will not go until tomorrow. The queen, quite properly, stays at home; but alas, the son will also make the attack presently.

I can also speak with feeling about my uncle and aunt, who lead a strange life. They are either going to the country, or moving to a new house, or being very, very ill. My aunt does not drink wine.

There is a great deal of trouble in my book. The family has a hard time. They get up *a las cinco,* which is five in the morning, and they eat stale bread and drink black coffee. Juan had to walk the streets five days trying to find work when he went to Mexico. Luis cannot take a trip because he has no job and no pesos.

And there is a nasty little brother, who will not study, will not work, spends his time in cafés, is always asking for money, and is really no good at all.

Even the automobile, which ran well yesterday, will not run at all today.

Poor Luis hardly closes his eyes all night, and cannot eat and has *dolor de cabeza* (headache) because his uncle died in Cuba a month ago. (Oh, those uncles!) His uncle was an outstanding character, the whole world loved him, but even so, I admit I was rather glad to see the last of him.

My poor aunt constantly *tiene los ojos llenos de lagrimas* — has her eyes full of tears; and you can't blame her when you think of what her life is.

And, as if there were not already trouble enough, the books which were ordered did not arrive, although some nice views of Mexico City were sent instead.

In the supplementary reading, there is an amazing story, which has a real moral. A certain Don Pedro came home late for dinner and the soup was cold, *fria*. In a regrettable moment of anger, he threw the soup out the window. Whereupon the servant, quite properly deciding to teach him a lesson, threw the rest of the dinner *por la ventura* also, together with the chairs, tables, dishes, forks, knives, spoons, and everything else that wasn't nailed to the floor. "It's a beautiful day," he said. "I see the señor wishes to eat outdoors!" Thoroughly chastened, Don Pedro went on eating cold soup the rest of his life and never said a word. This is one way of solving the servant problem. Don Pedro's man must have been an uncle of *The Saturday Evening*

Post's Hazel.

My adventures in Spanish have led me to think about education very seriously. Adult education, I believe, is the answer to a good many of the problems we have today. If every parent became a student for one night a week, for instance, there would be a new closeness to children.

And our own outlook would be broader. We tend to grow in on our own circumscribed world, and enlarging the horizon is a magic thing. Whether it be history, or philosophy, or how to plant petunias, no matter. It is a good thing to exercise our minds on something outside the routine of living.

Lectures at women's clubs do not fill the need. Soaking up culture like a passive sponge is a good enough thing, but working at a subject is better. The effort on a sustained program is rewarding. Most educational institutions have some adult education to offer, but even in small, isolated communities there are always specialists in various fields. Any group of women could find a teacher, wherever they are — an expert farmer, to teach out of his knowledge of the land, a factory engineer to discuss his field. Most high-school teachers, over-worked as they are, are generous with their talent if you are really avid to learn.

Then, too, there are the public libraries. They will give reading lists, suggest books. And there are records available for language study. They do help with pronunciation, and you can listen to them while you make beds or scrape carrots for the baby.

I'll take Spanish. Someday I may even be able to read one of the fine novels being written in Latin America, in the original!

The development of art and literature in our neighbors to the south is an inspiring thing to watch. Too much of the world is exhausted, and one might fear we would live in an era of blank-ness. And then the music and poetry and painting and fiction come fresh and vigorous from the South American coun-tries and Mexico, and it is a most heartwarming thing. The influence on the art of the dance is tremendous, too. Instead of looking to the Russian ballet, many choreographers are adopting Latin patterns now.

I had a new sense of the closeness of

peoples a short time ago when I met a young Mexican Indian who came to the United States to study. He spoke just a little English, and my Spanish was as yet unborn. I thought desperately, Whatever can we find to say? I tried to ask him what he was studying.

He was studying how to rebuild the land; how to reclaim the sterile fields on which the peasant population of Mexico slowly starves out its life. When I said that we, too, in New England were trying to learn how to feed the land, make the rocky fields fertile, his smile flashed, and by the time we parted we were intimate friends.

And now, when I see Jill bending over our rocky piece of New England soil, hoeing in all kinds of things to enrich the earth, I am thinking of the young, eager Indian, far away and down below the border, working, too, on soil rebuilding. Somehow it is a good thought. None of us is alone, all over the world men are kin to us. When everybody realizes this, war will be an old wives' tale.

The fifteen puppies (three litters all born the same week) are eight weeks old. I took a pan out to their house with their first fish dinner, canned mackerel. Two of them plunged in bodily and lay down in the fish in their excitement. A puppy completely imbedded in mackerel is something to clean up! A third puppy lost her balance and stood on her head, hind legs waving frantically. Finally the stern was righted and she came up, breathless but triumphant. There are always several who are like the children that announce at the beginning of every meal, "I don't eat much." They sit back, looking up at me. Then they take a slight nibble. They make a great to-do about it, lick their paws and scamper around, one eye on me. And generally, then, they nip in and get enough to fill their stomachs. And there are some who eat like an army on the march, gobbling vehemently until they can only waddle on fat legs. When they are as tight as drums, they collapse where they are and begin to doze, sleeping so as to get up an appetite for more.

The grown dogs consider them, on the whole, a frightful nuisance. Windy has a red son who is a miniature replica of him, and he nipped him severely for following him around. Pussy, on the other hand, plays with him like another puppy, and looks like one. She will never be anything but a puppy, not even after all the families she has had. Her own five and the other ten drag at her ears and stumble under her with equal pleasure. She plays a curious kind of tag with them, in and out, urging them on to tear after her.

Sister thinks nothing of them. Even her own puppies bore her after a few weeks. "Children don't amuse me," she says, with her nose in the air. So they like nothing better than to persecute her. They creep up and pounce, and when Sister nips them, they scream that they have been killed. In five minutes, they pounce again.

When the dogs eat, they have their own pans and they start busily with their own dinner. But after a little while they invariably shift. Honey will push her blonde muzzle into Windy's dish. Windy, after a single growl, looks up and runs to Honey's dish and eats rapidly. Meanwhile Clover and Bonnie have exchanged. Usually they circle like merry-go-rounds until all the bowls are empty.

I suppose that this is on the very human theory that someone else's meal is better than their own.

Needless to say, Star is no prey to this illusion. What's hers is hers, and let anyone put a nose in it on peril of his life! She is a supreme individualist and goes in for no form of sharing.

July is a busy month at Stillmeadow. The garden is very demanding. The crops are coming in.

I am really very fond of beans, both green and wax. But there are moments, as we pick on and on, only to have new ones ready by the time we reach the end of the row, that I really think the Luther Burbanks went a little too far. The Lady Bountiful is certainly well-named. We have millions of beans from every plant, and just as I think I can take a day off for something else, Jill appears with another basket of beans, which must be frozen at once.

July meals are no problem, because we may have as many as seven vegetables that should be eaten right now. And we all like chopped raw vegetable salad. A good piece of corned beef simmers happily with a mort of vegetables. By adding the vegetables in the order of their cooking time, you never have any squashy ones. Chuck or rump of beef is delicious, too, when simmered with vegetables, and it is an easy meal for a busy day.

Much as I love to cook — and I do love it — I hate to miss the fishing when the bass are running. I suppose they run, although they seldom run in my direction. Maybe they just run away. Now we have a small, very fat, very tippy rowboat, supposed to be carried on the top of an auto. It actually holds two people when it is launched, and if three get in it, it sinks almost out of sight. It rows equally well in any direction, even sideways. It is named G.L.B. because, as I said, it is short and fat and unmanageable, and G.L.B. were my childhood initials.

But how happy we are as we pursue a very erratic course up the Housatonic, round and round, and forward and sidewise. Old-timers fish up and down the stream, and give us avid inspection. They never have seen anything on the river like the G.L.B. Generally they are very kind, and advise us where to throw our lines.

But there is one boat, named Black Dan, garnished with a painted crow on the bow, that I always try to avoid. Black Dan is a sturdy large rowboat, and four weathered, experienced anglers belong to her. They fish in silence, two lines apiece, and double hooks on each line. They have, last word of superiority, a bucket of live bait over the side. They always find the only hole where the fish lie. The fish just fight to get on their hooks. Jill and I don't mind this, though it strains Don's love of his fellow man somewhat; we are glad to see a fish on anybody's hook. But these fishermen begin to hoot with laughter as soon as they see our boat. They lean over, and rock back and forth with mirth. After awhile we get upset by Black Dan's hysteria over the G.L.B. and its fishers. We row away, backward, forwards, side-wise, but very, very dignified.

Then, over the bass grounds, we drop our lines. If we get some good stout perch, it is fine; if we get bass, it is amazing. But we get the sun and wind in our hair, and the reedy smell of the long weeds, and the color of the water. We have the stillness, the long, dreamy stillness that lies only over wide water.

The G.L.B. sways and jiggles and maybe we get a bite. The excitement of that pull — the watching, the terrible question, "Shall I pull now, or wait until he nibbles harder?" The breathless pull, the abrupt jerk, and finally — is it a bass?

Then the sun goes down and the cool air spreads along the water. The banks grow dark, and the sky is peach. It is hard to see the bait on the hook. It is hours after we should have gone home. I see in my mind's eye the dogs, hungry, the puppies wriggling, the people who did not come with us looking at the clock every five seconds. The curious thing about fishing is that you never want to go home. If you catch something, you can't stop. If you don't catch anything, you hate to leave in case something might bite. There never is a time to stop.

Along the bank I once heard a frantic woman calling her husband, "Supper's ready, you've got to come in!"

"I'm coming," he answered. Then he rebaited his hook and sat on, placidly waiting. One more fish, that was all.

Finally it is too dark to see. The night boats are pulling out as we turn back to the dock. I am so cramped that I feel sure this time arthritis has won, and I shall never leave the boat again. This time I just can't stand up, let alone scramble up a verticle bank, carrying seventeen pounds of stuff and an oar, while Jill brings the anchor.

Our fish are never too heavy to carry, I admit. But as I turn for a last look at the dusky water, I am content. The intangible benefits of fishing have been granted me, and who could pack them in a wicker creel? I have been happy, happier than a mortal could expect to be.

"Let's come again tomorrow," says Jill. "I want to try farther up the inlet, in those weeds."

The warblers sang to me as I lugged in the firewood this morning. I wondered why they always come back to us from the West Indies or Venezuela. The hummingbird was over the border, and I know it must be my own hummingbird and no other. He acts as if he were

291

checking up on an old haunt. What strange, secret, hidden palaces, old as time, have these birds flown over, that now chat busily in Stillmeadow apple trees. Orioles from Colombia, cinnamon-colored wood thrushes probably late from Nicaragua. Places I shall never see — rich emerald jungles, carved stone porticos, incredible flame-colored flowers, purple and lemon orchids — my birds know them all.

It is strange how thoughts lie in the mind in different strata, like rock on a mountain outcrop. Sometimes I wish I could just plain think on one level, get it all dug up and over with. But I never can; just as I get well into a lovely lyric vein, I find a little idea has chipped into it, and there in my hand is a worry about next winter's coal; below that, I am still thinking about the canned ravioli I had for lunch, and wondering whether I could make it; and far down I suddenly find a day in my childhood, and my mother sitting down to rest briefly in the lawn swing. The lawn swing smelled of varnish, and the grass swished under the slat floor, and the seats were shaky.

I suppose everything that happens remains in the heart or mind forever — no doubt a psychiatrist could explain it all to me — but I keep on being amazed at the variety of feeling in a lifetime. One small, ordinary human being is capable of such joy, such grief, so much hope and despair and peace and conflict.

As long as there is a sky overhead there is beauty, something to live for. Early in the morning, when the birds begin, the light is an infusion of gold through my curtains. All the new insistent green of the world, and the glowing color from a thousand blossoms are in it, and the smell is so heavenly sweet it aches in the heart.

As I watched the early light I got to thinking about the nature of happiness; perhaps it takes a whole lifetime to become aware of it. We have it like a hidden pearl, or we have it not. It is something within ourselves. It is a quality of personality, and therefore no one human being can give it to another. We may surround our lover, husband, wife, friend with everything we can do for them, but in the end each man makes his own happiness in the adjustment of his personality to living.

This is the reason the happy people you know are often those who seem to have least. They are the mature people, who accept life and its limitations and still respond with a quality of joy to it.

I reflect further, if we cannot give it to people, does that mean that we should not do things for others? Certainly not. We should live every day so as to give the most to those around us. The best of life is the sharing of ourselves, the giving.

When I think of happiness I know, of course, that in any life there must be so much of suffering, so much of sorrow. Particularly in the world we know today, the sum of anguish beggars description. Our personal losses shadow forth the great loss of the world. But those who meet grief with courage have a kind of inner glow about them; their courage imparts strength to others; they are, in a sense, the happy people. For them there is no defeat in death.

The days go by too fast in midsummer.

"Summer's lease hath all too short a date." Every day I try to absorb all the sun and flowers and soft air I can, hoarding the memories against next winter. Sometimes I think the cockers do that too. They lie in the clean clipped grass under the maple, froglike, soaking in the good warmth of earth and smelling all the summer smells. Clover hunts forever for the squirrel she never catches. Sister and Snow help her now and then, but more as if they were doing it to cheer her up, than from any deep passion for squirreling. Jill says Clover ought to be raising another family, but she was ill with the last and has been retired. We are just too nervous about her to risk it.

Clover is the kind of female, says Jill, who runs up and down in front of the supermarket looking in all the baby carriages. Just like me, she means. These summer days, when we do get to the village for supplies, the whole street is lined with baby carriages. I never can resist running up and down and lifting the pink and blue covers and bending over the scraps of humanity. Usually they are asleep, so I can't tell the color of their eyes. Their bonnets are always over their faces, but a small tip of nose is visible, and two chewed bonnet strings.

With cocker babies, I am always reaching down and gathering up a warm wriggling handful. They begin to like it long before they have their eyes open. They snuggle in a lovely way, and make lapping noises, and push their noses under your chin. Cockers were just born to be loved, they say. Even the remote Honey works herself up into hysterics if I go off the place ten minutes and then come back, safe and alive and still sensible of her charms.

But Esmé gives me a different welcome. She swears and scolds and gives her tail scornful twitches. She has to be mollified by being asked to help open the paper sacks, and then, if she can get inside one and dash around in it, she will forgive me for leaving her. "But just don't let it happen again," she adds severely.

I remember July when I was a child. On the porch of our summer cottage was a swing with no back to lean against. It was more of a suspended cot, really, and I always wondered why the designers felt you could sit in one and just lean against air. But mother used to love it. After a hard day, she would lie down on that khaki affair with a brilliant hand-knit scarf over her shoulders. Green Bay was right at the porch steps, practically, and made soft sounds on the stone beach. Across the bay, the lights of the little village were lower stars in the night. Mother used to say that she wished her life would reflect only the lights, the way the water did.

So I see Cicely and Don and Dorothy moving around outside the range of the picnic litter, and I wonder what they will remember in years to come. Memory is such a fearful thing, if it is not wonderful. Will they remember scraping the crusty cheese from the casserole and seeing the soft light fall on our hills? Who can tell what little things will never be forgotten, what big things may be lost in time? Will they remember the time I made them scrub the kennels because they had shut all the doors and the dogs couldn't get out? Or will they remember summer picnics?

When we go to the shore to visit Don, who is a sailing counselor at Crystal Beach Camp, we stop at the old fish house and bring home all the fish we can. Clams, lobsters, fillets, swordfish, anything there is. We have had good luck freezing boiled lobsters, and ordinary fish is easy to freeze. We wrap it in freezer paper, seal with a hot iron, and rewrap in brown paper, to protect the cellophane underneath. Fish chowder we freeze in round containers.

Going to camp is always a highlight in our lives. We picnic on the way, stop off for a piece of milk glass or a Leeds plate in one of the antique houses and get to the beach. There is always that wonderful moment when we first see Don loping over the sand, looking so tall and so brown, and needing a haircut. And the fun of seeing a whole beach full of small, bouncy boys, from age six up to twelve. They are all over everything like a litter of puppies.

The salt water is cold, but feels wonderful. And the sand is as white as new-fallen snow. The Macs come out on the porch with the dog, and white sails blow against the blue sky, and somehow the world seems a fine and amiable place.

When we go back inland, the air seems

flat for a time, and the sun not so bright. And then we drive down our own road, and find coming home is a good thing, too, with cockers bounding inside the fence and Silver, as usual, outside the fence, trotting down the road to meet us. The cats just materialize out of thin air as we reach the steps. And when they realize where we have been, the strong imperative voice of a Siamese is heard in a state-wide broadcast about fish. We steam clams for supper, broil a couple of lobsters, cook a fillet for the cats, feed the dogs, wash the dishes, bury the lobster shells where Tigger will not dig them up at once, freeze the extra fish, and are ready to call it a day.

Honey lies on the terrace as we go out to see what flowers have come out during the day. The house looks dreamy and tranquil. The great maples that overhang it are deepening with shadow. A single star brightens over the meadow.

And Jill comes up with a basket. "We have to do more beans tomorrow," she says.

One test for me of good poetry is how sweet it sounds to the ear. I felt very

fortunate when I heard Robert Frost
read aloud his new book, *The Masque of
Reason*. And I immediately earmarked
my own copy to read aloud to anyone I
could find. Yeats is good reading:

"Down by the salley gardens, my
    love and I did meet;
She passed the salley gardens with
    little snow-white feet."

What a pleasant sound the words
make! And "The Song of Wandering
Aengus":

"I will find out where she has gone,
And kiss her lips and take her hands
And walk among long dappled grass
And pluck, till time and times be done,
The silver apples of the moon,
The golden apples of the sun."

I am very fond of the radio, and
nobody loves to listen to records more
than I do. But sometimes I think family
life loses something warm and close and
pleasant by never reading aloud in the
cool of the evening. In the pre-radio era,
even if the whole family was engaged

with different books, there was a kind of sharing. We ought to revive the custom of family reading, I think.

The meadow is very still and beautiful in the summer night. A silvery mist rises. The barn and the maple trees and the house look as if they had been dipped in melted silver, and the shadows on the lawn are laced with silver, too. The bright splendor of the moon transmutes the apple orchard into a place of dreams.

"Stay a little, summer, do not go," I whisper, as I take a last look around me before I go in.

August

Song for August

Love is a quiet hill that stands too high
For any valley eyes to estimate,
The violet peak belongs to stars and sky,
And Time against those slopes records no
    date.
The storm that ravages the lower way,
The cloudy snows that dim the valley view
Measure their transient armies for a day,
Scar not the curve that breasts the evening
    blue.

Having climbed now to breathe this upper
    air,
And set my heart upon the air-borne stone,
I have no need of downward way to fare
Back to that lesser land so long my own.

Never, oh never, shall I walk again
Breathing the dusty darkness of the plain.

WHEN WE FIRST came to Stillmeadow, there was an old covered bridge over the Naugatuck river at Seymour. It was narrow and rickety and set at right angles to the road on either side, so that getting across safely and into Seymour to shop was a delirious adventure. You just never knew. Maybe this time someone *would* be coming in as you turned out. The old boards rattled, the bridge shook slightly. But how I grieved when the bridge was torn down! I still miss it as we whisk over the broad cement span now. It was cool and dark in the old bridge and little slivers of light filtered in to make the dark more pleasant, and the air was damp from the river. Even crossing it in a car, you could imagine driving over behind a pair of horses, clop-clop-clop-clop. You could imagine all the people who had crossed the river in long-gone days. It was like opening an old book for a moment and looking into yesterday.

There is always something sad about change, even a change for the better. On the other hand, things must change, for there is no vitality in what is static. When I look at people around me, I sometimes think that when people reach the day in which they can see no good in anything different and new, on that day they begin to die. The will to live and the will to grow are the two foundation stones on which humanity is built. During all difficult days, I am determined to keep new interests going, lest I bog down in worry and anxiety. We need to use our time constructively, creatively, if possible.

This should be the month to lie in the hammock and read good books. For one thing, even in Connecticut, it gets feverishly hot in August. Of course, it cools off at night — it really does. This belief in the coolness of nights is universal in all people I have known, no matter what the climate. Everyone will admit they have very hot weather during the daytime, but "at night we always sleep under a blanket." I feel confident that in the very hottest spot on earth, the inhabitants would say that, while it gets warm in the daytime, at night they all sleep under blankets.

The heat has a shimmering, incandescent quality when August puts herself into it. The cockers like to go to the brook and throw themselves in, and come out to shake water and mud over everyone. As for the cats, it is almost unbearable to see Esmé sitting by the kitchen stove when the thermometer is shooting sky-high. "The Siamese like it good and warm," she says. Tigger sleeps in the sun on the terrace. His black fur is like a furnace. The black dogs feel hotter than the blondes and parti-colors, too.

This is the time they all want to dig nice deep holes under the expensive shrubbery on the terrace. The ground there is moist and very cool, and the evergreens shade them. They have dug up a large lilac in this manner, and two hemlocks seem to be rooted in nothing but space. Every night we have to rush around and carry fresh dirt to fill the holes, topping it with good heavy stones. For the worst parts we put up a length of chicken wire. This gives a really individual look to our landscaping. I feel sure

Stillmeadow has a special kind of appearance, not duplicated in any home magazine.

The houses in the magazines look so perfect; never a thing out of place, and the people, if any, sitting perfectly groomed and smiling on an immaculate terrace. The interior views are even more amazing. How fresh and shining every single object, how uncluttered the tables.

Sometimes I am irritated by the decoration experts. The last article I read was about a woman whose house was full of whimsey, said the writer. It was. It was simply bursting with whimsey, if by whimsey she meant a lot of impossible colors slung together and toned down with gilt and red velvet and dark green. When I reached the room where "the dresser had been whimseyed up with white and gold," I uttered a frightful sound and rushed away. Passing rapidly through the living room, which has no whimsey at all, I entered the kitchen and proceeded to whimsey up the stove by cooking perfectly plain golden wax beans and a panful of beets with no humor in them. I afterward scrambled eggs with chicken livers, and whimseyed up the table by putting on the knives, forks, and plates.

I love beautiful table settings in my favorite magazines. If I ever envied anything — and I often do — I would envy the fortunate housekeepers who can set up an entirely new table every time. Imagine having so many sets of china that every meal you can use a different color scheme!

With us, if the Bennets come to dinner, they find themselves eating from the very same set of dishes they had the last time they were with us. They undoubtedly recognize the tablecloth, too. Furthermore, as I look with the eye of a critic on our table, I admit to Honey and Esmé that all is not according to Hoyle, anyway. The dinner plates are modern, a pale soft glaze. Because we haven't enough antique ones. But the glasses are old thumbprint, some of them chipped. And the platter is my Wedgwood with the soft grey-blue pattern, so beautiful. The vegetables are probably served in French earthenware casseroles, which keep things piping. It's authentic Stillmeadow, and not whimseyed up.

Our breakfasts are usually rather sketchy, but we do ourselves well at night. In the morning everyone gets whatever he feels he wants. The thought of a big breakfast prepared for a lot of people who can't all get organized at the same time, fills me with such horror that I can't face it. My general attitude toward life when I first get up is of deep suspicion, verging on hatred. Breakfast in summer should always be eaten out of doors on trays, and with very little conversation. Whatever anyone has to say, I don't want to hear it.

Later in the morning my spirits resume their accustomed state and I proceed on a more or less even keel. I look on those people who bound up in the morning with zest and fervor, with awe. There are some; I have even lived with some. They go up like a slide fastener. I am simply basted together until after breakfast.

Oddly enough, most of the cockers like to stay in bed in the morning. Honey will roll an amber eye at me around seven, and then sigh and go to sleep again. None of this early-morning hunting for her. Star may get up and go hysterical when she hears the farm truck rattle by, then she wraps herself in a ball and sleeps soundly until the day is really begun.

Usually, day after day, I modestly have a breakfast of tomato juice, unbuttered dying toast, one piece, and black coffee. And then suddenly it comes to me that half a lifetime of breakfasts have already gone over my head. I rise up with battle in my eye and eat French toast with bacon, tiny sausages with fried apples. Or fried tomato slices, red and golden, on buttered toast.

Anyone can learn to cook. Jill, whose skill now rivals that of Oscar of the Ritz, one had such a reputation that the family looked with dark suspicion upon anything produced while she was in the kitchen. I remember one morning when I was sick, she whipped out to get breakfast. I heard strange clatterings and bangings and loud exclamations. The smell of smoke drifted in. Finally Jill came in bearing a tray.

"Sorry to keep you waiting," she muttered, red and breathless. "Everything kept burning up."

I could see that it had. A blackened object in the plate looked faintly like

French toast. There was a very overdone egg, its yolk broken.

"The egg just fought me," said Jill gloomily. "And every time I took my eye off the toast, it burned. I threw away four pieces."

She used to be very funny in the kitchen. She could wade in and do a mort of dishes with a rapid hand, and the speed with which she got the vegetables ready was more like a factory than a private house. But when it came to the finicky things, she was embattled. She suffered, and you could see her suffer. You could also hear her.

Her theory was that a kitchen should be run like an office in a large New York City organization. But a kitchen doesn't run that way. A kitchen goes by its own peculiar heartbeat. It can't be legislated, nor made to run by memos. It isn't a group of foods and implements and gadgets. It is a person, an individual. A woman who really loves to cook feels a funny little jump in her heart when she steps into her own kitchen and sees it waiting, herbs over the stove, pots and pans scoured and receptive, icebox a treasure chest of things Queen Elizabeth never tasted.

And a kitchen has so much significance now, in this world where millions go hungry. I think of the women in Australia, in England, in Canada, in France, in China, facing with me our common job, our common problem. The national health must, if possible, be maintained and preserved. Food is our responsibility, our charge. Think of women all over the world, quietly and faithfully carrying on their burdens. No trumpets blowing for them, perhaps, but the sound of a teakettle steaming cozily.

Of course I get tired of cooking. There are times when I wish I never had to butter another potato for baking. And I think one more dish to wash will be the last mile. Particularly when the house is so full of company that there isn't any place to sit down. And as soon as one meal is done, another comes sailing into view, inevitable, inexorable. It would be nice if all mothers and housewives could work on union hours and get one day off, I think. Imagine an eight-hour day for a housekeeper! Think of a whole day to read poetry and polish fingernails!

Silver has learned how to jump the picket fence. She has also found out that by going around the outside of the yard, she would end delightfully in the midst of the chickens. The first we knew of it was when a guest came down to breakfast and said, idly, "Who is the little black-and-white one that stays with the hens?" We flew out, expecting an end to our flock. And Silver was lying down by the chickens, just watching them with interest.

The strange thing about it is that when she is inside the fence, she rushes at them with everyone else, whenever they come near. All the dogs make a game of flushing the hens at regular intervals, and the hens give a few conventional squawks, and go on eating. Silver must have figured out in her funny little head that the chickens are part of the place.

"Well," said Dorothy, "I'm glad it wasn't Melody who got out." Melody is not noted for rigid self-control. In fact, she has a gleam in her eye when she sees Esmé lolling on the hearth. It really would be wonderful to play catch-as-catch-can with a cat, she thinks. Then when I say something about it, her eyes are as innocent as a spring day. "You misjudge me entirely," she says.

When I was in high school we had a dancing club — actually a dancing-eating club. To the inspiring phonograph records of The Skater's Waltz, and Ivanhoe Two-Step, we whirled blithely from the dining room door to the front porch, and back again. Everytime we got to the dining room door we popped in for a little nourishment. We even gave a formal. I must have been fourteen — I had braids flapping down my neck; in our little town braids went out with the war. I had flat patent-leather slippers, polished vigorously with vaseline. I had a rose-colored crepe with little pink rosebuds for a belt — it was just beautiful.

My escort borrowed his father's Tuxedo. He was a tall, broad-shouldered boy, but his father was rather large, too. The pants came down over Bill's patent pumps in little ripples. The trouser belt was nipped in oddly with safety pins. He looked like the Prince of Wales and Beau Brummel to my fond eyes; but unfortunately, in the middle of every dance, he was apt to get a glazed look in his eyes, break from me with a mutter and bolt upstairs. After the sixth exit I insisted upon an explanation.

"My shirt," he said unhappily, "my shirt." The stiff front belled out like half a barrel. He placed one hand on it. "It keeps coming up," he said desperately. "The pins don't — they don't —" and he bolted again.

The evening was a little jerky. I decided formal clothes were quite a responsibility. But when I really fell in love at the age of fifteen, I decided to dress up if it killed me. My poor mother, up to that time, used to wail, "You'd go out in a gunny sack, if I didn't watch you!" Suddenly I was changed. I went to the ultimate length of sewing fresh white collars on my navy serge middy suit! I have never forgotten the clothes I had that year. The pink ratiné two-piece dress with the flounce on the skirt. The ratiné stretched out of shape almost at once; I must have looked like a bag of potatoes. The corduroy suit trimmed with brown fur. The pale blue evening dress.

And I had a rose velvet evening bag

with powder and a puff in it! I carried it to my first formal banquet, and that was also my first public appearance as an after-dinner speaker. The staff of the high-school paper gave the dinner, and a solemn lot we were, seated around the long table at the Menasha Hotel. I had a lovely speech about the future of the publication, and I was going to read it. It was in the evening bag. I had been clearing my throat all day, and sucking lemons. I seemed to have swallowed a block of pavement during the night.

But there was a new boy sitting on my left. He had just come to our school that year; he was from away. It was all over with me with the soup. The dinner passed in a kind of dream, and I didn't even rise when I was to speak until he poked me nervously and whispered, "Get up, get up!"

I got up. I never even took my speech out of the bag. The bag was in his pocket, because he was "seeing me home." I must have delivered some kind of speech, but I shall never know what it was about. There was only one thought in my mind. "He's got to like me! He's got to like me!" Fortunately, on the way home, he said he did.

The poor boy led a stormy life from then on. I was feverishly jealous; I took it very hard. Romance didn't seem so easy as in books. If he walked a block with another girl, I was wretched. Once he even took a rival to a picnic. She had large black eyes, and black curly hair. None of us "spoke" for a week, and then I had it out.

"You will have to choose," I said dramatically. "Choose between me and her!"

I know now some adult sense of pity must have been wakened in him as he solemnly chose.

Here I am now, among the vegetables and the cockers, and farther from that little town of yesterday than any space. But I can still feel how terrified I was, how lost and desolate. Suppose he had chosen her!

When Dorothy reached the boy era, she was in a girls' school. She spent half a year trying to get Don, who is three years younger, to introduce her to the boys in his school. She said, slanting her eyes at him, "Now Don, if I should just happen to be in the yard, and the boys are there, what's the name of the big tall boy with blonde hair and blue eyes?"

"Oh, him?" Donald was bouncing his soccer ball. "That guy's Babe Ruth."

"Well," said Dorothy, "If I happen to be there, suppose you just introduce me to him."

"What for?" Don bounced the ball again.

"Never mind what for. You leave that to me." She spoke mysteriously. "All I want is for you to simply say, 'I want you to meet my sister Dorothy.' "

Don stared at her. "You want me to get my face pushed in?" he asked. He was disgusted. "Do your own introducing."

"But I can't — You'll simply have to —"

"I'll get my face pushed in," he said with finality. "Then the whole gang'll sock me."

There is never enough time to read. But how precious is the hour that is winnowed out of the day when one *can* read. I like to read aloud, but only to an attentive audience. I like best to read aloud two things: poetry, and pieces like

Clarence Day's *Life with Father,* or James Thurber's *My Life and Hard Times,* or Saki's short stories. Novels are better read alone. Ordinary fiction should be read by one person at a time. But poetry or brilliant sketches make ideal evenings.

Not long ago my Virginia friend and I got to quoting poetry. We matched bits. When we missed lines, we helped each other out. It was a lovely evening. She began with an old-time favorite — "Here's a sigh to those who love me, and a smile to those who hate" — so we did Byron for half an hour. "The isles of Greece, the isles of Greece! Where burning Sappho loved and sung" — on through the love lyrics, "Maid of Athens, ere we part" and "She walks in beauty, like the night"; bits of "Childe Harold" and "Don Juan."

We were practically drunk with George Gordon, Lord Byron, before we moved on into the intellectual ether of Keats with "I stood tiptoe upon a little hill" and the magnificent tones of Shelley's "Ode to the West Wind." Some of the lyrics we stopped over: "Rarely, rarely comest thou, Spirit of Delight!"

and the lovely "Music, when soft voices die."

Rupert Brooke, Sassoon, Millay, we had to get down the books now and then, due to our mutual habit of forgetting the last line of the octave in a sonnet. But we ranged high, wide and handsome until the night was a sliver of moon in a thin sky. Then I realized, coming awake in the "dead vast and middle of the night" that Cicely was still up, hands linked around her knees.

"Mercy on us," I said.

"My goodness," said Cicely, "who knew *you* knew all those poems?"

Administering this coup de grâce, she moved off to bed, while I, nothing but a parent, let the dogs out, let the cats out, let the dogs in, let the cats in, and crept to my middle-aged sleep, while outside the summer night was still full of stars and dreams.

When I pick golden wax beans or cut the rhubarb chard, I wish someone had devised a way to grow vegetables on shelves. Leaning over in the hot sun is not my idea of comfort, and I never have been able to adopt the stance that is pictured in the beauty pamphlets.

Jill, however, is never really happy standing upright. The crouch position seems to be her favorite. She goes along on her knees with her nose practically in the earth. When I see her out among the lettuce, I feel sad to think that she has had to spend so many years in the city, being what is called "gainfully employed." If there was ever a born dirt farmer, it is Jill.

What I like is berrying. Up the hill to the old pasture land on a summer day, with an old lard pail hooked to my belt — that is something. The pasture is full of blackberries and nobody takes care of them but God. There they are, rich purple-black, and smelling of sun and summer. They fall in the pail with soft plops, each one a perfect little nugget of goodness. The pasture grass is short and green and the old grey ledges are warm in the sun. The lichens are beautiful and the spring runs cool in the hollow.

You can hear the neighbor's tractor on the opposite hill, and it is a comfortable sound. In the soft mud at the edge of the spring are the narrow, delicate prints of deer.

Better than the blackberry pasture, however, is Blueberry Hill. We had to live here long enough to become natives before we were permitted to see it.

My feeling is that when Heaven was being made, somebody cut off the selvage, and it fell down, and this is it. Incredibly remote, the acres of blueberries stretch for literally miles — open land, tight thickets, deep shadowy wood, hot steamy swampland, and all of it full of blueberries.

From the high places, you see half of Connecticut rolling below in a green and tranquil sea. The white houses look like small boats at anchor, safely moored. Distant hills take on a warm blue tone, almost like the blueberries. There is usually a faint haze, delicate and dreamy. It begins to deepen around the middle of August, when the late berries ripen.

In the thickets you see only interlaced branches making a green gloom. Deep moss stills all footsteps; only the voices of the berry pickers come faint in the silence. The high bushes are here, with ripe and unripe berries at the same time. The unripe ones are waxy — first a pale jade green, then a pearly color.

The blueberries have a spicy smell; the tips are like little fairy crowns, and they are perfectly enormous. We pick until we can hardly lift our hands, and the pails hang heavily from our belts and have to be put on the ground. Cicely feels the same way about it that I do, and never wants to stop, no matter how late it is.

We have big bowls of blueberries for supper, dusted ever so lightly with sugar. Pitchers of cream for those who can ignore calories. The next morning we have blueberry muffins.

I use this recipe: 2 cups flour, 3 teaspoons baking powder, 4 tablespoons sugar, ½ teaspoon salt, 1 cup milk, 2 tablespoons melted shortening, 1 well-beaten egg. Reserve ¼ cup flour and dredge 1½ cups of the berries in it. Mix dry ingredients, combine liquids, and add quickly to dry ingredients. Drop by spoonfuls into buttered muffin tins and bake twenty-five minutes in a hot oven, 450°. This makes twelve muffins, and is enough for three ordinary people, so it must be doubled for our brood.

We eat most of our meals in August outdoors. It seems a shame to miss a single hour under the dreamy summer sky. The barbecue is in constant use. I love to have supper about sunset time, cooked over the fireplace, and then, as the embers glow redly, sit and feel the cool of evening coming softly over the meadows. There is a kind of quiet in a summer evening which is like nothing else in the world. It is quiet like an opening golden rose. The sky is the color of moonstone after the sun dips behind the green hills, and later on it is lilac and deep purple. Then the summer moon silvers everything over, and the stars unfold their petals, too.

Conversation ebbs away on such a night; people sit dreamily, the last flicker of fire lighting up a man's pipe, a woman's clasped hands, a child's eager eyes. Melody is a piece of night itself, and Esmé and Tigger, who love the barbecue, sit happily on the stone ledge. Esmé's eyes are opal, Tigger's are topaz. We always linger until the damp mist rises from the swamp and the last ember falls apart.

This summer, whatever conversation goes on is practically always on the subject of plowing, or not plowing. After reading Mr. Faulkner's *Plowman's Folly*, Jill began to think we were ruining our soil by the cultivation and turning. Then we got Louis Bromfield's *Pleasant Valley*, and decided we should never plow again. My natural conservatism views the idea with some distrust, but Mr. Bromfield is a most persuasive man. I do believe that the future of America depends on the richness of the soil and that we must stop letting it all flow away in the rivers. Also, commercial fertilizer dumped on is not enough to preserve that lovely layer of topsoil. The level of our own vegetable garden, which is flat, has sunk several inches just since we began to use it. Now the gardeners are spending extra effort, carrying chicken litter and moving in compost to help out, and we shall extend the cover crops this fall.

Neither Mr. Faulkner nor Mr. Bromfield mentioned one thing, as I remember it, and that is the wonderful effect of burying garbage in poor soil. Our land is very erratic, as most New England soil is. One end of the garden was once practically useless. But we began burying the garbage there, and now that end is better than the other. The Indians never knew how intelligent they were to bury fish heads in the hills of corn.

The new theory of cultivation involves disking the soil instead of turning it over with deep plowing. You merely chop it up, plant, and the old refuse, which was once so carefully burned, enriches the soil and keeps moisture in it.

I think the war made America more conscious of the value of this great, naturally kind land. But we must preserve the heritage if America is to continue to be the land of the free. We need a new race of pioneers, pioneers in rebuilding worn-out land. It is a very pleasant thing to think, as we steer the wheelbarrow-load of chicken litter through the interested cocker crowd, that we are doing something for the future, as well as for this next garden.

Jill is considering the idea of geese. So far we have done very little about livestock. We always bog down on the idea of raising things and then having to kill them. Even the hens, that should have been fricasseed long since, are still clucking around. Probably we might do better with geese, but I doubt it. Another book started her off on this idea. This is Mr. Ed Robinson's *Have-More Plan*. But the Robinsons are practical folk; they have rabbits and goats and a pig. One seldom thinks of a pig having much charm, but one of my friends got a pair of little porkers to raise and by the end of the season she was taking them out for walks every day, and they followed her around like puppies. In the end, she had to take a trip while the pigs vanished.

It is easy to feel the goodness of the earth in August. Full summer dreams on the fields. Through the hot days the farmers are still haying. When our neighbor fills the barn, the chaff makes a haziness in the air. It has a golden quality. The heat itself is strangely exciting, and the richness of harvest stirs every sense. No one can believe God is not good when the August gardens are in their heyday.

The big golden moon makes night so bright that the dogs are apt to get barking sprees in the middle of the time they should be still.

When the dogs really get in full chorus, nobody can sleep. I have to get up and go to the back kitchen and switch on the kennel light, and speak harshly to the dogs that are in the house. The kennel will become violently silent as I switch on the lights. All the dogs rush inside and sit looking at the light in surprise, and this stops the noise. But not permanently.

If it is around two o'clock, I can't get back to sleep. All the assorted worries that any woman acquires wait to pounce on me. I worry about the world situation. I go into anguish over the possibility of not being able to pay next year's income tax. I feel perfectly sure Cicely will marry some no-account man who will be an albatross around all our necks. Dorothy will be misled by some charmer who dances well and has the brain of a hubbard squash. My sinus and arthritis and a lot of unknown diseases will do me in within a week or so. There will be nobody left to make popovers for the family. The dogs will miss me. Nobody else, I say, thumping my pillow, will care. Somebody will ruin my washing machine and somebody else will turn the stove on in the well-cooker and burn the precious aluminum out.

These and other two-in-the-morning thoughts keep me occupied for some while. All those dandy little articles on not worrying run through my head, to no avail. I know I should think of pleasant things and relax, but I can't think of any pleasant things to think of. I relax so hard that both pillows fall under the bed and I have to get up and fish them out. My mind goes like an electric mixer on high.

Summer is almost over, but I prefer to think so in the midst of sunlight and the brimming garden, not in the night. Nobody should ever say good-bye to summer in the wakeful hours of the night. Better to take the blow while the zinnias make a flare of color and the cosmos are beautiful in the sun, promising that there will be another summer.

One reason that August is so tranquil is that it is the season between lawn-furniture painting, and storm-window putting on. The vegetables will grow and ripen, now, whether they are hoed daily or not.

Even the lawn relaxes from its feverish growing, so the lawn mower can rest a day. Fall cleaning is just a distant prospect and spring cleaning just an old wives' tale. Nor do we have to worry yet about gathering wood for autumn. We are content with a small fire of fallen apple branches in the late evening.

Or if it is a still, hot night, we pile in the car and drive to Eight Mile for a swim. This is best of all, perhaps. The dark water lies so cool under the white moon, the woods are mysterious, filled with faery folk, light-footed and shadowy.

To be tired and hot and dusty and come to a woodland pool and swim in the cool, sweet water — what a special gift from life!

When we are gone, back to the little white farmhouse, and the cockers are taking up most of the room on everyone's bed, then I often think the faery folk are coming out of the woods. They ride the ripples on water-hyacinth leaves, and they feed the smallest silver minnows. How wonderful is the world on such a night!

And Honey says a down pillow is fine

for a golden girl's head after a very busy
day guarding the house.

Yes, August has its own charm.

September

Song for September

Not that I ever had her for my own,
Quick in the house I heard her running
  feet,
Watched the door swing, garnered a
  sentence blown
Back to my stillness, "Friends I have to
  meet."
Nor that I knew her, never her secret
  thought
Came home to me, nor how she dreamed. I
  knew
Each growing year the size of clothes I
  bought,
And that her favorite sweater set was blue.

Now sober reason counsels me again,
This was not yours that goes beyond your
  sight.
Knowing this well, I must perceive with
  pain,
The bough is empty when the bird takes
  flight.

Bravely my mind assures me nothing's lost,
But oh my heart admits the killing frost.

THE WIND IN the sugar maples has a different sound. It is the sound of summer's end. Anyone who has ever heard it would recognize it. I think that if I ever, like the poet, "met a traveler in an antique land," and we talked of homelands, the wind in September in New England might be one mutual pleasure, no matter what the climate.

September wind blows away the fatigue of summer heat, and the listlessness of August weather. It blows away, indeed, the piled up years. It makes the heart young. Going back to school, football games, dancing, falling in love, corn roasts, moonlight rides — so many such things belong to September.

I always feel that something fine is about to happen. And the fact that winter is on the way is not troubling this early in autumn. Time enough to think of that in October and November, but now it is too soon. First comes the harvest, the last ripening, the splash of zinnia color in the garden, the perfect late golden rose. Yes, a good time to be young, and to relive young days.

Clover and I got greatly excited this morning over a baby owl that was huddled doubtfully in the maple near the house. The mother owl, from a tree near the barn, was trying to persuade her offspring to come with her. She did her best, and on the ground, Clover added to the furore. The baby owl seemed to be a confused sort of person, and he couldn't quite decide to get off the branch and try the deep air.

Clover and I had to go in the house, and when we came out again, both owls were gone. But there was a humming-bird quivering in the perennial border, incredibly bright, and incredibly tiny. We seldom see one, and I wanted to move as close as possible. Above all birds, the hummingbird gives me that feeling of the mystery and the wonder of life. Such a vibrant little body, such color, and wings that beat faster than thought. I felt as if I could watch the whole of life if I could hold a hummingbird in my hand once.

But as I stepped softly nearer, a bright unafraid eye seemed to inspect me briefly, then the wings quivered and the bird was gone.

The orioles are gay in the old orchard branches. The swamp is full of birds, but I can't get out in the middle to see them. Their liquid notes make the air sweet, and they are all very busy. A beautiful male pheasant came along the stone wall yesterday, stepping proudly and glittering with bronze and purple.

How sweet are the country sounds! Keats was right, as he generally was: "The poetry of earth is never dead. . . . The poetry of earth is ceasing never." The soft tapestry of bird songs comes first, then the sound of water running cool under dark branches, the creak of a wagon deep with hay, the fiddling of grasshoppers; all the good country sounds make poetry.

Snow's puppies come out on the lawn now to tumble in the sun. Snow is bored with them; she wants to stay in the house. Time for them to go away to boarding school, she thinks. Supplementary feeding has made super puppies of them.

They rush to the feeding pan now, and lunge into it, swimming happily in egg and milk. They make excursions into the vast, vast world. The grass is very tall for them, it is hard work to get around in it.

Now and then the boy, filled with male ego, gets way off, and then discovers he is alone. He is a voyageur in unknown country, and he lifts his voice and adds to the summer sounds the desperate wail of a lost puppy. Woooo-Woooo-Wooooo! Everybody drops whatever he is doing and runs to fish him out of the rose bed. Then what joyous reunion, what snufflings and pantings and lickings and waggings as he settles his fat self in the rescuer's neck and yawns.

The first meal of scraped beef is always a celebration. The babies are dozing in the sun when I come out and hold a fairy-sized meat cake under a sleeping nose. There is an instant convulsion through the whole litter and they all fling themselves violently at the luscious smell. "Why didn't anybody tell us about this? Why didn't we get this before? Where is more? Gracious, you expect us to live and grow up on mush and milk?" Long after the meat is gone there are smacking sounds, then finally they give up and fall asleep, paws in air, fat stomachs turned up to the sun.

A mad dash after a paper hanger brought me inside a kitchen where soup was being canned. The lady was a big blue-eyed Swedish woman with that open, steady look which real Scandinavians always seem to me to have. The kitchen was sweet with dusk and supper and pails of fresh milk, and the blended odors of soup.

While we visited, Mrs. Larsen went on washing dishes, her hands expert and careful with the worn pans. Now and then she came over to the big range and slid a fresh chunk of wood in. The light from the fire shone on her face. I longed to be able to draw, to catch the modeling of strong bones, the firm, kind mouth, the level sweep of eyebrows.

"It came to me to can some soup today," she said.

She was canning in a water bath. She said she boiled the soup about "two hours or so," then packed it in the jars and set it in boiling water in a big kettle to process "about an hour or so" longer. It seemed a miracle to me, who always cans soup with a stop watch in one hand, and an eye on the clock, to boot.

I had gone in with a very sad heart, but when I left I was marvelously restored. Just a clean, simple kitchen with a wood stove and a quiet, kind woman, and the Connecticut hills outside the window deepening to violet. I hated to go; I wanted to rest in the peace there for a long time. I stood on the stone stoop while she hung up the clean steaming dish towel. The men came walking from the barn, silhouetted against the last light, and the smell of hay was in the air. I felt the earth turning under my feet, and I felt the goodness of life above and under all the sad things.

I did not get the paper hanger.

That Tuesday was a day. It began with a frenzied chase for a plasterer to patch the walls in the upstairs bedrooms. After an hour of search I ran one to earth by a tennis court outside of Seymour. He thought he could make it by Thursday, he said. Then the furnace man came from Waterbury to adjust the furnace for winter. I finished a half bushel of tomatoes. I can them in their own juice, pressing the tomatoes down until the juice flows over them. While the pressure cooker was on, I fed the dogs. Then I took in a small washing I had done somehow, earlier in the day.

At five o'clock I continued the hunt for a paper hanger. This led o'er hill and dale, until I wondered dimly how anybody ever finds time to hunt foxes, when it takes all the time there is to hunt workmen. If I had had a horn, I might have sounded a tallyho from the hilltop, just to keep in the spirit of the hunt.

I got home around eight, moved bureaus, chests, beds and chairs madly, wishing the family had not all gone to town. This was a futile wish, too, because we were doing over the bedrooms with the idea of getting it done quietly while nobody had to sleep with head pillowed on wet plaster and feet covered with wallpaper paste.

Well, I thought, I am going to bed this minute. I won't even bother with my favorite radio programs. Just bed. I gave Honey a snack and let her out. And let her in. Let Tigger out and let him in, took Esmé out of the china closet, and had just crawled into bed when the phone rang.

"Hello," I managed to say feebly.

"This is Mr. Wububub. I'm in Newtown," said a voice, slightly indistinct, due to the peculiarities of country phones.

"Who?"

"I've come up from Stamford with those pine boards," he said. "Where do I go from here?"

I was dazed. Driving from Stamford?

He explained. "I had to make a trip for some stuff of my own, and I can't make but one trip your way. I'm going on up to New London."

We had long since given up the pine boards as lost.

I said, "I'll have to meet you at the Triangle. You'll never find the place in the dark." I told him how to get to the Triangle.

"I'll be there in ten minutes," he said.

I got dressed. I got the car out. I drove to the village. I remembered Jill mentioning months back that she met a man at a dinner party in Westchester who had some antique boards from a town hall in Vermont, and Jill had happily bought them. So here they were, at nine-thirty at night! Pine boards, indeed!

At the filling station our bachelor neighbor dashed out. "Hello," he said.

"I'm meeting some pine boards," I said.

"Old pine? There," he pointed, "that's it! Must be."

An enormous limousine swayed around the curve, wearing a complete wrapper of pine boards. Boards twenty feet long, and heaven knows how wide, clattering and sliding and trailing clouds of old comforters behind.

"I got lost," said the driver. "I seem to have gotten off on the Bridgeport road. It's so dark."

"I shouldn't think you'd try to deliver pine boards at this hour of the night in a strange place," I ventured to say, as I led him toward Stillmeadow.

I held a flashlight while he tried to untie the ropes. The spaniels set up a fearful din, not being used to night deliveries of pieces of old town halls, right under their noses.

Finally we got back in the house, and I prepared to pay him. The phone rang. "I just thought I'd call up," said Jill.

"Just to see how you're getting on with the rooms. Would there be any place to sleep if I brought a guest for the weekend?"

The September rains are something I just live through. The rain falls straight and dark and heavy and the leaves on every tree and bush are beaten down by the weight. The early-turned leaves are lost now. The rain seems sad, meaning the end of summer days. No comfort to think, now, that the garden needs it; the garden is doing very well as it is. It reminds me of other rain, in other Septembers.

I thought of you in the rain last
  night,
For there is isolation in the falling
  of rain
Like the memory of you invading
  my brain.
You are there, not clear and
  bright,
Not shadowless, nor warm with
  sun,
But striking me with the terrible
  beat of rain,

When the rain has just begun.

To break away from melancholy it is better to stop peering out the window to see how much harder it is raining, and how dark the sky over the meadow is, blackened pewter now. If you lean out, the air is as hard to breathe as if you were swimming under water.

This is the time to build up the fire, even if it is not cold. The leaping ruddy flames give a brightness to the dim room and the heat dries the air. A cup of hot tea and a toasted biscuit with cheese bubbling on it, are cheering.

I don't see how this month can be so exciting and at the same time so sad. It is like the second-act curtain in the play of summer. And every day you feel like begging the play to go a little longer, before the floodlights go out, and summer is gone.

But there is excitement too. The dramatic first flame of maple, the burning gold of the goldenrod, the coming of the first blue wild asters and the richness of ripening pumpkins. Even the air seems to have color in it; one breathes the color, and the heart beats with it.

I am always frightfully sentimental now. Whether the second-act feeling is responsible, or the color goes to my head, I don't know. But I really go all out with sentiment. I wonder if all women — and all men too — can possibly get through this month without a sneaking glance back at their school days.

Getting children ready for school must bring back the days when the middle-aged parents were slim young reeds swinging off to high school with the world an opening rose in the hand. Every single September of my life I walk down a certain street of my childhood, under maples as flaming as these, carrying Twelve Centuries of English Literature, Vergil, Advanced Algebra.

One lovely thing about the return to school was the delicious realization that I could see the boy I was in love with between classes and at recess and at noon and walk home after school with him, and yet not get into the same delicate situation with my parents that I was in during vacation, when it was quite evident to their eyes how much of the time I spent either with him or getting ready to be with him or thinking about having been with him. School was a great comfort.

Now I have to reflect how many of the boys in that class in school are lying under the soil in France. The ones that came back have now lost their sons in another war. These are the things that stay in a woman's heart. In September, the month for going back to school.

And yet, when the sun comes down in the garden and the sky has the soft delicate look of coming autumn, I cannot help feeling that we must defend our land, now, tomorrow, years to come. And so, when I think of the boys I knew, who went out from Vergil and Algebra so long ago, I still know they did not go in vain. Even though, twenty-odd years later, I stood on the street with a flashlight and an arm band watching the sky for bombers.

I wish we could put up this late summer sunlight in jars. If we could only pack it, clamp the bail down on the glass, set the pressure cooker for, say, ten pounds, and process jars and jars of bright, fresh, mellow sun! I can see how it would look with the jars ranged in the fruit cellar beside the chicken and piccalilli and tomato catsup. And on a dark January day we would bring up a quart or so of sunshine and open it and smell again the warm dreamy air of a late-summer day.

Now that autumn is practically here, we begin to look at the diminishing wood pile and plan our trips to the woods after fire material.

We acquired some wood this month at a fearful cost. A small private hurricane descended on us, and in ten minutes took down all the old apple trees in the back yard. Wind and rain made a roaring darkness around the house. A window crashed in and water poured clear across the room, and presently the electric cables to the house were reft away and the place plunged in darkness. The intensity of the hurricane had a curious effect upon everybody. It was terrible and dramatic, and when the great black walnut went down across our road, like a falling leviathan rolling into a deep sea chasm, nobody had any words to express it. We were such little unimportant creatures, ant-small in the midst of it.

It was over suddenly. The air was like pale silk. In the sky the clouds boiled away. We went out, and the neighbor boys appeared. The girls volunteered to walk to a phone; they disappeared, and turned up later saying they couldn't get through the road. We had a cold supper by the light of a few candle ends.

Meanwhile the boys came out and mounted the walnut with axes. In the semi-darkness, they swung the heavy tools, striking sparks, and cut a passage through. By ten o'clock the Connecticut Light and Power emergency crew was on hand and, by a floodlight, hooked up temporary cables. It was an inspiring sight. After the devastation of the hurricane, these men proved all over again the ability of human creatures to combat disaster. Up in the tangled branches, around swinging live wires, working in the night, they got the service on. Then they cheerfully went away, promising to come back in the morning and rebuild the whole line.

When day came I looked out on the back yard and felt sure my heart was broken. All the lovely old apple trees, so sweet with bloom in the spring, were sprawled on the grass. Only two were left at the edge of the lawn. The hand of the storm had split the trunks in half, and the yard was so tangled one could not even walk across it. But the boys came over from our neighbor's farm, and a group of boys from the girls' crowd volunteered to help, and the sound of axes began again. They worked all morning, college boys and farm boys, and by noon the worst was over. The college boys were blistered, but the farm boys weren't even breathed.

By the time I had got over weeping and emerged from my room, it was time for dinner. So we fed fourteen ravenous people in the barbecue. We took everything we had in the house and made a hasty picnic. In spite of the tragic loss of our trees, we recovered enough to enjoy the young people and their gaiety. The college boys gave most of their attention to the farm boys, admiring them wholeheartedly for the way they could cut, saw and fell dangerous split trunks. The girls meekly passed the bread and jelly and sliced meat and salad to the obviously superior sex. It was a man's day.

The cockers didn't think much of the hurricane. Windy does not like anything changed; even chairs out of place in the house make him nervous. Honey is allergic to repair work; men up trees is a thing out of nature, she feels. Clover and Snow jumped up and down and screamed because they wanted to come out and play too, and we had to keep them in for fear a tree would crash on them. Saxon and Sister were divided in opinion. Maybe it was a celebration they should be in on.

When George, the farmer, came to blow out the stumps, we all got in the house and clustered around the windows. Don was pleased as Punch. The process was a work of art. The charge of dynamite went in just so, and over all went a large laced pile of branches, deep and thick. The effect was like an air-raid shelter, camouflaged. The fuse was laid carefully, the fire touched to it, and there was a boom that shot Star nearly to the ceiling and sent Honey under my bed for the afternoon. Almost lazily the whole mass rose in the air, the stump disintegrated, and a hole was left like a dry well.

One large root sailed over the house and landed in the lilacs in front, which Don thought was simply marvelous.

The cats just make themselves scarce when anything strange is going on. Nobody would know we had a cat. But after things quieted down, Tigger inspected the whole terrain with Esmé flashing around him like quicksilver. They decided it was a fine thing to have a hurricane, because when the trees came down a number of small creatures were blitzed. I was roused early the next morning by Esmé trying to bring a squirrel in bed with me. I do not like squirrels in bed.

The world was particularly tranquil after the storm. The sun had a clarity and brilliance and the sky was very deep and pure. The drenched earth glittered. Even the garden, with everything battered and drowned, had a peaceful look — all passion spent, as it were.

I went down the rutted road. It was a day for a hopeful hum, and I began to sing to myself a little off key, as always — but the spaniels think I sing beautifully.

Esmé and Tigger came along behind

me, tip-tipping delicately. When we went by the old black walnut, Esmé skipped up on the trunk and peered at me with sapphire-blue eyes. Before the storm the tree was too great for her small brown paws, but now she could run up and down with ease.

I was about to go into a mood over the significance of this when Don came bicycling down the way. "Hi," he said, "Cicely wants to know is there anything in the house to eat?"

So we went back to see if there might be any food at all.

September is a wonderful month to work outdoors. The fresh cool air is invigorating, but the sun is still pleasant. The last canning, preserving and freezing must be done. It is time to check over the fruit closet and the freezing unit to correct any oversights. We have used up all the home-baked beans, the cookie dough, the frozen soups and casseroles which we did early in the year to save cooking in the heat of summer. It is a good thing to have several meals assembled in the freezer, ready for unexpected company. If we put down a pot roast, cooked, a container of gravy, rolls, and cake, we can add frozen asparagus, spinach, corn, or beets, and have a meal. Jill makes extra batches of brownies when she bakes, and they are perfect when they come out of the freezer later on.

It is not too late for my favorite soup, vichyssoise. Most cold soups leave me cold, so to speak. They just don't seem natural to me. I was brought up on soup so hot it burned your mouth. But the vichyssoise is delicious. We use Colonel Murray Edwards' recipe, which he served me first in Lexington, Virginia. Perhaps the memory of the violet mountains against a pale sky adds special flavor to my enjoyment of this soup.

It calls for 2 cups of raw diced potatoes and two cups of raw diced onions cooked together in a very little water and put through a fine strainer. Feeling the way I do about putting things through strainers, it has to be worth it, and it is. Then you add 1 cup of chicken broth, and when cool, 1 cup of smooth sour cream, and beat well. Season with Worcestershire sauce, salt, chill, cover with chives, and serve in cold bowls.

If I have no chicken broth I use chicken bouillon paste or cubes. I find it takes about 2 cups of water for the potatoes and onions to cook soft and not burn. This is a good soup for meatless days, because it is rich and satisfying.

It is time to think of fall cleaning. I know all about the new scientific way of doing one room at a time the year round and never doing the whole house at once, spring and fall, but I ask myself, Then when is the house all done? Think of never having that blissful moment of sitting down, aching and worn out, to be sure, but finished! The other way is too much like never dressing up entirely, but putting on one fresh thing each day. I'd rather give myself up to the business, all in one fell swoop. But I do admit it is a help to get the closets out of the way ahead of the main attack. And the desk drawers. And do on a rainy day all the odd jobs, like fixing the broken curtain rod and cleaning the elbows of the dogs' favorite chair.

But the real fall cleaning must go until the dark weather. The September roads are calling, glorious with goldenrod, blue with chicory, red with swamp maples. The real way to use time now is to pack a basket and climb the hill to the old orchard and with a few cockers hunting madly up and down and around and about. A small fire will fry new-laid eggs until the edges crinkle, and split buns will toast. If there is a bit of bacon, the meal becomes Olympian. A picnic is always better, too, with what we call "dibs and dabs" — a bowl of cottage cheese (with olive oil stirred in until it is soft), dill pickles with a faint tinge of garlic, red-currant preserves, celery fresh from the garden. Coffee is best made on the spot, and cookies or little cakes make the easiest dessert to manage.

After the picnic is over, the family can range the woodland beyond the orchard, gathering dry fallen wood to carry home. Or sit in the warm sun and read poetry — poetry that is dreamy and still and bright as music —

"O for a heart like almond boughs!
O for sweet thoughts like rain!
O for first love like fields of gray
Shut April buds at break of day!"

I like to read aloud almost anything of De la Mare, for his words are strung with enchantment. And I think he is the cockers' favorite poet, because the sound of the music is pleasant and lovely to sensitive ears.

"The scent of bramble fills the air,
  Amid her folded sheets she lies,
  The gold of evening in her hair,
  The blue of morn shut in her
   eyes."

Honey ought to like that one especially, with the gold of evening in her own hair. And Snow has golden ears, too. When sunset comes, the cool air flows over the orchard, and it is time to rake out the ashes, pour water on them, and go home. Everyone can face the next day's hard work better for an interval of serenity. I read so many articles on nervous tension and anxiety and fatigue these days. People have been strained too long beyond the natural stresses and strains of living. My recipe for trouble and knotted nerves is simple, but it works. Go on a picnic on a cloudless blue day. Sit on the warm, rich earth that mothers us all, let the soft wood-cool breeze blow in your hair. Eat everything you can hold. Read a little poetry. If possible, take a couple of dogs along.

City people can picnic too. One of the best picnics I've known was on a Brooklyn roof, with the great river dark silver below and the lights of New York coming slowly out against the blue of evening. There was chicken and a green salad and rye bread in a basket, and it was a beautiful picnic.

When I am away from Stillmeadow and come in sight of the little white house again, I must have a certain expression on my face. For Cicely always says, "Yes, Mamma, it's still there."

I expect this sums it up pretty well. The feeling a woman has for her home place. The drudgery that goes with housework, the never-ending labor that is involved, the tiredness, the routine — clean, wash, cook, clean, wash, cook — how easily all these slip from our hearts in a single moment of realization. Possibly no words could be more sweet to the heart than these:

"Yes, Mamma, it's still there."

After supper last night I went out under the apple trees to look at the moon. It was one of those hours I have when the world is so lovely I can hardly bear it. All the rich and beautiful things there are come home to my heart at once. Sensation is an ache. If there were nothing lovely but the deep serene evening sky, that would be enough, I think. But there are the trees, heavy with leaves, there are the roses opening in silence and beauty under the moon.

There is the grass itself, strong enough to bear the heavy feet of mankind and yet to grow, to be mowed, and grow again. There are the vegetables, and every one different, a whole world of taste and texture to bless the hunger of man. I am almost dizzy thinking about how the crisp cabbage can be so different from the melting sweet of ripe tomatoes; how the golden tender wax beans grow beside the sturdy round onions with their compact rings, translucent and heady.

As if that were not enough, sounds assail the ear with mystery and magic. I heard a fox bark on the distant hill. I heard the soft stamping of a horse in the neighbor's barn. I heard the brook.

Color alone would be enough of beauty for the world, I thought, sitting down on the terrace. Surely it would take all my life to have enough of that pale, pale green that sometimes lies along the horizon when the sun has gone. Or the cool dark amber of brook water over stones. Or the faint ivory in the heart of a white rose.

A thousand textures have their burden of beauty too. The smooth suave feel of a petal rubbed between the fingers, the softness of a spaniel's coat, the hard good sensation of a stone in the hand, the incredible feeling of a cobweb, which is hardly texture at all but the dream of texture. Wool and silk and ivory and ice — the mind cannot call them all up at once.

Scents — there are the special evocators of memory. Almost any smell will bring a whole train of remembered hours with it. Violets — one whiff of violets carries me magically back to a field of violets I walked in twenty years ago. Smoke of burning leaves — a whole enchanted autumn lives in that odor. White sweet clover —

All this physical beauty of the earth is not half, either. Music and poetry, the remembrance of things past, love and friendship — all the infinite riches of the mind and soul itself are spread for us as we move through the world.

A cool wave of air from the heart of the meadow came to me and I filled my lungs with it. I turned back to the house, white in the moonlight, and I thought, Yes, in spite of all, I am in love with life. There is more beauty than we can measure in this old world of ours. There is surely more beauty than we can measure in a single night.

Blue is the color I love the best, and blue is September's color. Blue skies, softer, purer blue, blue gentians, blue chickory by the roadside, blue grapes in the arbor, and over everything that dreamy blue haze that comes over the woods at twilight.

The second late blooming of the dark delphinium comes now, too, just before the frost. Of course the leaves begin to turn, and the harvest fields are a thousand tints of gold, but in New England October is the month for rioting color and in September summer lingers on past the mid-month time.

There is a kind of enchantment about a tranquil blue morning. I feel as if something wonderful might happen at any minute; and on the other hand, the day itself is a wonderful happening. Warm, and yet not hot, cool enough but not cold, this is really the way weather should be, I tell Esmé as I get breakfast.

"Siamese do not care for the cold," she says, stretching a brown paw. "Personally, I'll take the hottest day in August and sit in the sun and be really comfortable." But Tigger is an all-weather cat. He is just like the inscription on the post office — Neither wind nor sun, and so on, can stay this swift courier from his appointed mouse.

The cockers will take September as their month, but they would live in an igloo and break the ice for their drinking water rather than be two yards away from the family.

Oh, lovely blue haze, drifting over the upland pastures! Oh, still and misty meadow! Oh, dreamy September sun, riding at anchor in the blue, blue sky!

"Think not of spring, thou hast thy music too!"

October

Song for October

Now singing colors chord their trumpet
   tones,
And maples make bright music up the hill,
The brook runs amber over polished stones,
The pond is deeper than the sky, and still.
Come the late wagons rumbling down the
   lane,
Freighted with pumpkins, cabbages, and
   corn,
Wheeling the dust into a golden rain,
Leaving behind the ravished fields forlorn.

Sweet summer is again a memory,
And lyric April a lost fairy story,
This is the season of the singing tree,
The winding horn of Autumn's ambient
   glory.

Only my love for you with Autumn glows
Yet keeps the pattern of the budding rose.

THE SPECIAL GIFT of frosty gold days comes now; time to lay down the household tasks and shut the door on routine. For every October, when I see the trees over the meadow, I think, "I shall not look upon her like again." And every October is different, strange with new beauty.

With old gunny sacks over our shoulders, we climb the pasture slopes. Here the outcropping ledges are warm and grey but have delicate colors laid over the stone, pastel of lichens, rosy-tipped, soft olive, copper-tinged. The pasture itself is still green, a muted green, and all the goldenrod and chicory and wild asters spill more glory over the stone fence. As if this were not breath-taking enough, "I will lift up mine eyes unto the hills" and see the sugar maples and oaks and butternuts. There should be new words every October for the colors gold and scarlet and bronze and russet. There they are, living fire, and a re-establishment of God's good will to earth.

We go up to the farther lot, where the butternuts have their tawny leaves lifted against the soft sky. The nuts are cinnamon or black-suede color, and the long ovals hang in delightful clumps together. One kind of rain that I like is a rain of butternuts plopping on my bent head.

We fill the gunny sacks and then wander on to the hickory trees. The green-lacquer covers of the nuts split open easily, and inside the pale polished nuts are hidden. A hickory nut is beautifully made, with its delicate ridges and tiny point to finish it off. It feels smooth to the hand and has a faint pleasant smell. I love to roll a handful in my fingers as I gather them.

It is still and peaceful up here, and the air has a dreaming quality. When we have wandered as far as we need, for the gunny sacks do get heavy very soon, we move to the biggest ledge of all, where there is a nice flat place to spread a picnic supper.

The menu is an old one, for this nut gathering has all the aura of tradition with us. New-laid eggs, fried crisp at the edges and just firm in the golden centers. Slices of dark bread to lift them on. We have big ripe tomatoes laid on grape leaves, to eat in the hand with salt and pepper.

And this is all, for we can't carry much when the nut sacks are full. Usually we find windfall sweet apples near where we eat, and make dessert of them.

When we bring our nuts home we spread them to dry on clean papers in the storehouse. They should dry well and have the outer husks removed before being hung in bags from the rafters.

Another crop is ready for gathering, too — firewood. We take a wooding expedition and bring in old dry fallen branches and broken limbs, chop them up and stack them for those open fires. We always mean to get enough for all winter, but we never do. Because there is the vegetable garden needing last aid, and the perennial border to clean up for fall, and the kennel to scrub and paint. Every day is bursting with things to do.

The real countrywoman wishes she were triplets in autumn. There is no limit to the amount of work, except that in the end, one's feet turn to rubber.

On rainy days, instead of resting, there is the lawn furniture to spray with paint, the tools to clean and oil. The cellar is piled high with debris, and where it all came from nobody knows.

The woodshed must be filled at odd moments. Almost any hour of the day passers-by, if there were any, might enjoy the sight of me pulling a child's wagon from the woodpile to the kitchen door. We use the wagon for moving heavy groceries from the front gate, too, and for carrying things to the barbecue in summer. I really don't know how people keep house without a wagon.

It is still warm enough in the morning to eat breakfast outdoors. The grass is frosty, but the sun on the sheltered terrace is like golden wine. The smell of hot coffee in the clear air is extra fine, the marmalade looks amber, the hot rolls melt away.

Sometimes I ask myself a little uneasily what the first owners of the house would think. By the time we eat, they would have had their washing done and no doubt be churning butter. They made soap, dipped candles, wove their own flax. Perhaps the old woman was right who said, "Tain't like there was plenty time anymore like there used to be. Even with all these new fancy clocks, time is mighty sca'ce."

I wish I could make our own bayberry candles. It would be nice to burn them on winter nights and have the scented smoke bring back our own October gathering.

I wonder how much we ever really enjoy anything we have put no personal effort into. If we wove cloth, for instance, we should remember the long bright days of spinning, and the air and sun; and the sound of the wheel would all be in it, the songs we sang, the food we ate that time, what everybody said, how the puppy ran away with the wool. A whole warp and woof of memory would be there forever. But now a piece of cloth means only how tired my feet were and how hard it was to get waited on in the store.

But Jill points out this sounds very well, but I wouldn't have patience enough to weave an inch of anything. It would drive me crazy, she says firmly.

Jill is so annoying when she is right.

We have been cleaning up the yard. The fallen leaves are never burned. There's nothing I like better than the smell of burning leaves, either. It reminds me of frosty blue evenings after football games, of corn roasts on stone ledges over-looking the waters of a dark river, of moonlit fields. I am docile about giving up the romance of burning leaves in favor of having good fertilizer for the peren-nial border and a mulch for the roses. But I like to ride over the country roads to the village, where less sensible folk are raking great heaps of scarlet and gold and rust, where blue smoke rises soft against the sky and the heavenly scent comes strong and sweet.

And I often think how pleasant it would be if I could rake up all my small dead hopes, my faded illusions, and burn them like fallen leaves, and then begin with the clean boughs again in spring. A far more suitable time for New Year than the calendar time.

Yesterday I had a new experience. Our neighbor up the road has been raising a baby pig, and the latter suddenly developed boils. I went over to help take her to Dr. Beere. Having taken cockers over frequently, I thought nothing of it; I simply said, "I'll help you take Bunty over."

We had a small chicken crate, with no top, and a nice white piece of old bedspread to wrap her in. Bunty is a white pig, with a deceptive air of innocence and docility. We got in the pen and made sweet sounds. "Here Bunty, come here, Bunty." Bunty retired to the hay and peered at us. As we approached, she darted out and nearly tripped her owner.

"Come, Bunty, come on, Bunty," she coaxed, moving over. Bunty was almost there, and then she wasn't. And for the next forty minutes two large grown women and one small white pig flew around the barn like windmills. If we got our hands on her, she screamed death and disaster and smashed away. We tried dropping the crate on her, we tried doing a bull-fight act with the cloth. Once we got the cloth over her and she flew through the air like a balloon, cloth and all.

All the time she screamed as if we were murdering her, and this made us nervous. Her owner tried feeding her and Bunty would come up and whisk up the food all right; but the minute we made a nearer move she was off again. In the end we had to call in the farmer across the road. It took him about three minutes flat to have her in the box. So it seems there is technique even in pig catching! We felt very humble as we loaded Bunty into the car. "You have to sneak up from the rear," I said, wiping my red face, "and cling to a hind leg."

All the way to Waterbury Bunty screeched like a madwoman. And she rocketed around in the crate like a full herd of buffalo in a stampede. At times we thought the car would fall to pieces. Bunty's owner was so distraught she drove all over the road.

When we finally got to the doctor's and crawled out, he was standing on the steps of the office.

"I've brought my pig," said Bunty's owner.

He came around and looked in at the feverish eye of Bunty and then his eyes began to twinkle. Then he looked at our disheveled selves and began to laugh, and he laughed until tears were in his eyes. "Have any trouble?" he asked mildly, when he recovered.

We rested while he fixed the patient up and innoculated her and loaded her back, and then we drove home and had another unsuccessful bout with pig stubbornness, trying to get Bunty out of the small opening in the box. After half an hour more, she was finally hauled out. Panting and exhausted, we stood by the pen, and Bunty stretched herself out on a nice soft bed of hay and relaxed.

"Well," we said, "we're lots more tired than you are!"

Farming, I decided, is so full of technical skill that I wonder how anyone ever learns to be an expert farmer in one lifetime. If pigs are so difficult, think of cows and sheep and horses and chickens and all the other life on the farm needing special treatment. And as for the rest of it, I have not yet been able to wield a scythe and not make scallops on the hay.

In the early days building a house was an arduous task, but nobody worried much about plans. I often look at Stillmeadow and see the simple, sturdy lines of the house, the clean sweep of the roof, the arching maples now burning against the deep blue sky. I see the fringe of cockers around the terrace, and the cats, elegant on the picket fence.

And at the same time I see a spring forest here, deep with ferny green and tangled briar. I can hear the sound of chopping and the fall of great trees as the land is cleared, and the smell of fresh-cut logs for the cabin that was to be in this same spot. As the sun struck through the green deeps, I know how she felt, the first woman to have her home here. I can see her clearly, standing beside me, plain and slender in her homespun and with peace in her eyes.

The first cabin had one room, and maybe a lean-to. The requirements were simple. A kitchen, in which they lived and ate, kept warm and carried on household tasks. One could do without bedrooms, parlors were for later days, but a kitchen was primary. The kitchen was as large as a man could afford, and the great hearth was wide.

Now the kitchen has undergone a most marvelous transformation. Yet I believe in keeping the best of the past, and I do think a kitchen that can be lived in is a fine thing. Our house, built around 1690, may have been the second or third or fourth built over the cabin site, but it is old enough to have the great fireplace with the crane, the Dutch oven, the three-legged spiders for frying over the coals, and the stone hearth laid from hand-cut blocks.

The kitchen, now remodeled to the heart's desire, was one time two small rooms. When the job was finished, the back kitchen, or summer kitchen, simply insisted on "a bit of fixin'."

Many old houses have this large room behind the real kitchen, and many have woodsheds attached to the main kitchen. Almost anyone who has any kind of big back room, I think, would do well to remodel it into a real summer kitchen, for the advantages are countless.

Here, for instance, you may have the old black range, so comfortable, and so good for canning or baking. On cold fall days before the furnace is on, a quick fire in the range warms the downstairs nicely. Here, on boiling days, you may simmer the roast and keep the main kitchen cool for salad-making.

We have always used ours, but only after the main kitchen was made perfect, did we decide the summer kitchen must be made equally efficient and labor-saving.

The room is large and runs up to the roof. We put windows all around and windows near the ceiling to let in more sun. The walls are covered with insulation board finished with clear waterproof varnish. They are a warm honey tone and will stand any amount of wear.

It was easy to put in a sink and hook up the washing machine by putting them on the same wall as the inner-kitchen fixtures. This sink is first aid for everything. Garden vegetables are washed here. Gardeners can wash here, too, and not track in two tons of moist earth over the rest of the house. In the deep bowl the cockers take their baths, and small hand-washing is done. The washing machine is at the left, neatly fitting the corner, so we almost have a laundry right there, and the back door is at hand, so the washing can be carried out easily.

We had scrubbed the kitchen floor until we were worn out, and the impact of the front-kitchen remodeling completed its devastation. So we laid good strong linoleum, in a rosy tile pattern which would not show pawmarks too much. For a room with lots of traffic, this tile pattern is perfect.

Next we enclosed the sink, making room for the vacuum cleaner underneath. Falling over the spare parts of the cleaner has worn us out in the past. We put enclosed shelves over the washing machine for soap powder, bluing and other cleaning supplies. And a long narrow shelf over the sink for those extra cans of milk and dogfood.

One corner by the range made room for a coat closet, and the other now houses brooms, mops, dustpans and wall brushes. Any woman who has a family can appreciate how maddening it is to have the whole family stream in the back door and dump galoshes, raincoats, old hats, Mackinaws and baseball gloves on the nearest chair.

We lined the two remaining walls with cabinets and covered the tops with linoleum in a marble pattern that blends with the tile on the floor. We made the cupboards the height of the window sills, so that the work surface is the right distance from the floor, is perfectly lighted and is convenient for any job.

The wall to the left of the range houses extra canned and dried supplies, a tool kit for household repair jobs, and a dusting kit, packed into an easy-to-carry tin box. On the opposite wall, one cupboard is a bin for dry dogfood, and the next one holds the mangle, electric iron, pressure cooker and Dutch oven. This takes care of the oversize equipment, which does not belong in the main kitchen anyway, and needs to be kept out of the dust and dirt.

We used a white frill at the top of the windows, and let stencils on the side casings provide color and gaiety. This makes for more light, easy cleaning, room for the house plants in winter and a free sunny view of what the cockers are up to in the border.

Almost any woman would be happy with a supplementary kitchen like this, and many houses would provide one with little effort.

Our remodeling of the back kitchen was very inexpensive. We used scrap lumber for the cabinets, and when they went in they were very odd and patch-work-like, but with three coats of soft green, they looked like the pictures of before and after in the magazine advertisements of glamour schools. Some of the cupboard catches we dug up in the barn, the rest were the cheapest kind available. An old-fashioned open sink looks modern with the homemade enclosure.

The linoleum we did not try to lay ourselves. It will get the hardest kind of wear, and had to be cemented smoothly over the big expanse. The counters needed metal edging, too, to keep them trim and easy to clean.

A special feature for Stillmeadow was the Dutch door between the two kitchens. The door is knotty pine on the elegant side, and Jill put a broad strip of copper flashing on the other side for the benefit of the cockers. Now we can keep the bottom half closed if the spaniels are in and we are trying to cook dinner. They can bounce against the copper, receive handouts, and still not trip the cook when she dishes up the gravy.

One counter is just right for flower arranging, with the containers handy and the sink convenient for water and cutting. And the same counter is convenient for giving milk of magnesia to cocker puppies.

Small carpentry goes on here, too. Our remodeled kitchen makes it possible for one person to stir up an angel food cake for a birthday and another person to sand something down, and yet be sure there is no sawdust in the fluffy white icing.

With all the different kinds of things that go on at Stillmeadow, we find this arrangement makes for the happiest kind of living. But I have become such an enthusiast on the subject that the first thing I ask anyone I meet is, "What is your kitchen like?"

This is Esmé's birthday month. She prefers a nice dish of chicken for her birthday celebration. I remember so well the day we first saw her. We went to visit the royal Siamese family of which she was the liveliest, not to say wildest member.

We had been talking about the idea of annexing a Siamese for some time. "But the cat books say cats ought not to be moved around," said Jill doubtfully.

"And you know we would have to take her places —"

"Sylvia got along all right going to Michigan and back," I pointed out.

Sylvia was a charming cat, just a plain alley cat but with a lovely disposition. She turned out to be a male later on.

There are two kinds of Siamese, we learned, the seal point and the blue point. I wanted the seal point, being enamored of seal in any size or shape. At the place we found Esmé, there were two grown cats and the litter of four babies.

Siamese are born white, and these were still faintly creamy, though their noses and bootees were brown. They were not pretty, far from it, any more than an oriental carving is pretty.

Their bodies were thin and lithe, their tails longish. They raced about, and climbed and jumped, or stared solemnly out of large blue eyes. They gave one an immediate impression of their independence, wisdom, and shrewdness. I picked up the nearest one and looked at the porcelain blue eyes and my heart just turned over as the eyes looked back. "Their faces are just like pansies," I said, "brown and gold pansies."

"Pansies on very lively stems," said Jill.

Something ages old and strange and mysterious was in that small pansy face. I remembered cats are called "panthers of the hearth."

The owner tied a string around the stomach of the one we thought we wanted, but in two seconds the string was off. Esmé didn't like stomach strings, she said. The next instant she leaped on the radio, a good four foot take-off. Then she swung lightly up the curtain and landed on my neck.

Now I knew all animals were different from one another and cat nature is not like dog nature. Jill worried about this; she wanted me to understand that no cat would give back to me the passionate selfless devotion of a spaniel. But I told her that I had already a dozen passionate devotions in fur and I wouldn't be too frustrated if the cat did nothing but sit around being beautiful.

"You talk all right," said Jill darkly, "but I know you. You'll work on that cat and work on it, and if it doesn't act crazy over you, you'll feel terrible."

"I've had cats before," I said.

"Not Siamese," she said. "And you'll want to wash her, too."

"I shall certainly wash her."

We thought of calling her Saki, for we wanted a nice faraway name like temple bells ringing, and golden bracelets tinkling and jasmine and hot white nights. And like the nice line

"Like her, O Saki, you shall pass,
  Among the guests star-scattered
    on the grass."

And then we thought of H.H. Munro's Esmé, and looking at our darling, we knew she had no other name.

Esmé is the most verbal creature we ever acquired. It took some time to get used to her piercing Siamese tones, but now that we can follow her conversation it is all right. If we leave her, she greets us with a stream of Oriental phrases which are pure swearing in any language. At mealtime, or when she thinks it is mealtime, she begins on a questioning note which rises and rises until the meal is served, when she utters a last strangled word and falls to. If she is just

385

chatting, she ends her remarks with a question, "Wa-all?"

Tigger is a Connecticut Yankee, with all the stability that implies. He minds his own affairs, gets what he wants, and although he loves Esmé deeply, he refuses to give up his independence. In spite of all she can say, he goes out at night on his own business, and when he saunters in, hat under arm, Esmé falls on him with mingled tears and kisses. In fluent Siamese she addresses him, cuffs him, chews him, and then licks his fur nearly off in a burst of adoration. He turns an amiable eye on her, and at last licks her in return. Then they both fall asleep by the fire, arms around each other, all forgiven.

In all the little country schoolhouses soon the children will be learning verses, and especially "October's bright blue weather!" I used to sing it in a lusty tuneless voice: "Octoburr's bri-ight blue weathurrr —" I never could stick to the tune if anybody near me sang alto; I hopped helplessly from note to note, retreating into what I fondly hoped was the tune whenever the alto sank too low, then bounding out again on a safe middle tone. When the tune rose, I had to give it up entirely and follow along in a monotone yards below.

When Cicely was still practically a baby, she would come in and sing a whole song at the top of her lungs. "You like that?" she would say.

"Yes, that's fine."

"Well, I'll do it again. I'll do it in my flat voice next."

I suppose what I sang with was my flat voice. Later on, in college, I was trying to join the chorus of a beautiful sorority song, pitched high on the theory that high notes aspire to Heaven, I dare say. "I can't sing high C," I explained desperately, "I just can't!"

"Well, just get as near it as you can," said the president comfortably. So I did; I got up as far as possible, and then let go. I'm sure the effect was startling.

The days have been bright this week, but the nights have been silver. It feels so warm at noon that I can't believe the black frost will come at night. We pulled the last tomato vines and hung them in the back kitchen, where the tomatoes continue to ripen. We can still dig carrots, beets and turnips, of course. The chard keeps green almost until the snow covers it.

I have always canned all the chard I had time for, and it was never enough. It took me a long time to learn how to can it so that it wouldn't shrink in the jar. And just as I learned to blanch it long enough for the first shrinkage to be over and done with, and to run a knife down the center after the greens are packed, we got the deep-freeze unit, and forever gave up channing chard. The frozen product is infinitely superior in flavor, texture, and appearance. And the job is a thing of the past, once the blanching is finished, for packaging takes almost no time at all.

Gone, too, are the days when we canned summer squash, processing it for three hours in a water bath. Now we freeze it already cooked, either plain or as squash creole, and it is ready to serve as soon as it is heated. The first year we planted squash we were garden beginners. We planted a nice long row, and we had wheelbarrow loads. It got so that every passer-by was met at the gate with a carton of squash. I served it stuffed, scalloped, mashed, steamed, and in vegetable casseroles. For a while I canned far into the night, every night. My New England ancestry wouldn't permit me to waste any of the lovely delicate things, but I admit I had all the squash I wanted for some time.

This "season of mists and mellow fruitfulness" — how I love it! The apples are falling in the yard, the windfalls, the persistent fruit of the old trees that are never sprayed. Goldenrod and wild asters brim the lanes with color and light ebbs softly over the harvest fields. Leaves drift down, the maples are scarlet.

> "Where are the songs of spring?
>   Ay, where are they?
>   Think not of them, thou hast thy
>   music too, —
>   While barréd clouds bloom the
>   soft-dying day,
>   And touch the stubble-plains with
>   rosy hue."

I often wish I could see Tahiti, that I could know the South Sea Islands. I feel a nostalgia for places I have never known except in thought; for jungle rivers, swift and wild, for white coral beaches, for lustrous tangled vines and steep pale cliffs. I wonder if every woman does not, standing on her threshold, wish now and then for the remote lands below the wind. I should like to see the whole world before I die, I should like to reach the other side of the horizon. I should like, very much, to see a wombat and a panda.

And yet, where could I go to find more beauty than in these New England hills? Drifting blue haze over the woods, long light over the tawny fields, the wild-rose haws bright in the thicket, the coppery purple of blueberry bushes in the swamp, leaves drifting down, drifting down in the blue twilight — beauty to spare for all my needs, in my own place.

And who would think that I should prefer any living thing, near or far, to a golden spaniel with amber eyes and a soft deep muzzle? Autumn — "Thou hast thy music too."

Jerry is so big now and so swashbuckling. He digs the deepest hole any dog ever did. He lugs the biggest bones the farthest. He gets the muddiest. Exuberant, gay, optimistic, he is the kind of youngster that you laugh at while you fend him away from the pile of fresh laundry on the table. He loves everything and everybody. He is one long, constant hurrah.

Little Sister and Linda are old enough now to play with him in his roughhouse fashion. These two are adorable, and different as two people can be. Linda is smooth and black and large-eyed and cuddly. Little Sister is so busy all she can stop for is a lick or two as she flies past. She is the first one through the gate, the quickest at the food bowl. Of bones she gets the largest; Linda can have what's left.

We often think Big Sister had something to do with sending her to comfort us for the never-failing grief of being without one who was so much the heart of the place. We seem, in a strange way, to be given Sister's baby days all over again. And when we reflect that in all these years of dog raising, this is the first time we have had a puppy exactly like another, we should not be blamed for having special feelings about it.

Life renews itself, no matter how much we may suffer. Whatever beautiful and precious we may have is always ours to keep. Losing one we love is possible only if we let it be. Death and disaster, separation, and sorrow seem sometimes so much larger than all else, but they are not. Death really prevails only when we walk with him.

For supper tonight we had a main baked dish of sausage and scalloped potatoes, a green salad mixed at the table, grilled tomato slices to give a variation in color and taste and, for dessert, hot gingerbread frosted with cream cheese.

For the main dish I washed and peeled six potatoes, sliced them very thin, and put them in a buttered baking dish of moderate depth. I placed them in layers, and sprinkled each layer with salt, pepper and a little flour. Then I nearly covered them with milk and baked them thirty minutes in a moderate oven, keeping the pan tightly covered. At the end of this time, I removed the cover, placed link sausage over the potatoes and baked them another twenty-five minutes, uncovered, until the sausages were nicely browned. The potatoes were crusty brown around the edges, and the sausage juices made up for using no butter. Thrifty and good.

We like to keep cooking easy at this time of year so as not to miss any of the pageantry of color outside. The cockers feel very gay and they tear around in the fallen leaves with free-floating ears and shining eyes. There is a lovely stillness in a fall afternoon. Up in the pasture one can really "busy the heart with quietude." The stillness has the sadness of passing summer, and yet it has a breathless quality of life still to come before winter sets in. All the color that flames in the woods and runs along the horizon is so beautiful that it comforts and warms the sorrowful spirit. While the world continues to be troubled and the atom bomb is apparently the god of all things that are, I stubbornly refuse to despair. There is still love in the world, and kindness, and faith. So let us not abandon hope.

These days I like to go out in the woods with Honey and Silver, and consider the miracles about us. The leaf of the wintergreen is a small miracle, tiny and carefully polished and edged with faint silver. Beyond, in the open pasture, the hickory nuts are falling, and the sticky green-brown burrs of the butternut lie in small heaps.

The sunlight has a mellow tone, like the sound of an old bell. And with all the warmth, the air promises cold weather soon.

When the sun suddenly reefs her golden sail on the sea of day I feel the loneliness, for standing alone and thinking may be a lonely thing when the light is gone. At such a moment, it is a fine thing to feel a golden muzzle pressed into one's hand, and to see brown cocker eyes looking up earnestly.

Silver is panting from rabbit hunting, and says, "There is much to do, the woods are full of exciting things, why do you stand here on this rock?"

Yes, there is much to do. But the doing will be better if we remember all the good things there are under the infinite canopy of the sky.

Postscript

SOMETIMES I GO away by myself, up the hill, far enough from Stillmeadow so that I only see the slope of the roof almost lambent with sunset. Honey may pad along with me, for she does not disturb the aloneness; after all, Honey is only me, myself, in golden fur and with amber eyes.

From the upper abandoned orchard the yard is partly visible, dotted comfortably with cockers and cats, and if the weather is right, Jill's bent shoulders appear at the end of the tomato vines. If there are guests, and there usually are, the sound of their voices comes dreamily from the open space where the lawn furniture is.

If Cicely is home there is music, too, the sweet nostalgic sound of "Borrachita" or the one about the Aztecs coming down from the great white mountains to be slaves. Don is never visible to the naked eye, for he finds the best way to get through all the murder mysteries is to keep out of sight. Too many errands may turn up.

Dorothy and her new and charming husband, Val, will be working on their car; just married, the excitement of being together pitches their voices high and sweet. They bought a car named Carrie for a hundred and twenty-five dollars when they were married, and Dorothy says she spent her entire honeymoon in junk yards while Val tried to replace broken parts.

There is always much activity going on around the little farmhouse. Maybe Harriet Fitzgerald is painting one of her serene summer canvases, and the sound of a hammer indicates that her sister Ida is building something, either a new chicken house or a trestle table.

Somewhere, someone is forever pounding a typewriter; the sound of the typewriter never ceases at Stillmeadow.

There it all is below me, this little world within a world, and I sit down on a warm grey ledge upholstered with feathery lichens and think about it in relation to the rest of the world.

The terrible suffering that man is

undergoing all over the earth is like a tidal wave to overwhelm civilization. If we think of this, what can we find in the whole round turning earth to make any life good?

The intolerance sickens the soul. Race against race, caste against caste — by what dreadful arrogance could I believe myself better than another woman because my skin is pale?

But here in the country, we may establish one small territory dedicated to love instead of hate, and possibly that is why we were born. And just possibly when all men have homes, hate will diminish all over the world.

For we are always pursuing happiness and security. We pursue them, not knowing what they are. Now and then, rarely, we find them, if only briefly. But for me, and for many women like me, and for many men, a small home in a green valley is security and the opportunity to make a happy life.

Looking down on Stillmeadow I see the years that have gone, and the mark of them is a good and kindly mark, for the trees have grown, and the lilacs are spreading graciously. When nature devastates the whole yard full of old and lovely apple trees, she begins new life the next season with young maples, and that year the mallows are as big as full moons.

The seasons change but new life is always coming, and in the country one never looks backward. As soon as the crops are harvested, we begin to plan next year's garden. When the rose is faded, there is pruning to do for another lovelier rose. Moments of sadness when the delicate amethyst and ivory lace of the lilacs die may shake the heart, but on the morrow we go out to the border and see the rosy red peony, like an English country maid in a lyric, spreading a full skirt.

If I were a wise woman, I should understand many things about life which I do not now understand. Maybe I would know why there is so much evil walking the highways, why men must suffer, why the governments operate like kaleidoscopes instead of like good blueprints for living. Maybe I would know why "Im Wunderschönen Monat Mai" is just as German as Hitler and the concentration camps. And why the delicacy and purity of a Japanese painting is just as Japanese as the Death March. And why an educated kind mother can say, "Just don't go overboard on brotherhood, Gladys. Everybody is out to exploit us."

I think about all these things, up in the old orchard with Honey's muzzle soft in my hand. And about the first people who owned Stillmeadow's forty acres more or less. What dreams they had of a fair world with liberty and justice for all. What they and their sons died for at Ticonderoga and at Valley Forge and later at Bull Run and Gettysburg and what my generation died for on the beach at Anzio and at Bataan and in the Battle of the Bulge.

And suddenly I know. I know there is a dream that will not die, and that Stillmeadow, in a small and quiet way, is an affirmation of that dream.

And all the years we have been repairing the fences and painting the woodwork and doing over the old chest of drawers and getting puppies to lap their cod liver oil and picking the everlasting bean, the years we have picnicked and ached with poison ivy and dug up boulders and carried water and fed the hens — these years have a meaning beyond the actual small meaning of life lived in the Pomperaug valley.

The time we had seventeen adolescent guests and the time the puppy swallowed the bass lure and the time the freezer went off and the time when the coal gave out and the electric went off in January. The time we thought Dorothy had appendicitis and the time the cow tramped down all the broccoli and tomatoes and eggplant. The time we nearly burned down and the time the oil heater smoked until the dogs were all solid black; and the time the two hurricanes ripped part of the roof off and tore out the condensers, and the time lightning made an exploding ball at my feet.

All of these times were life at Stillmeadow.

And in my heart, too, is a goodly portion of death. The death of those dear to us, and the death of the loved companions who looked at life from the eyes of a cocker.

On the hill, with crushed fern beneath my feet, I remember Rip, gallant and noble and steadfast, a gentleman cocker with a heart as big as any need. And

Dark Star, who was a very feminine, erratic little black girl, and Sister, who was a lady, and Clover who was too good for the world. And Tommy, the musketeer, and Donna, the one who died at eleven weeks. And Static, who was poisoned. Ah, yes, I remember them, they are in my life still, they were Stillmeadow.

I remember my mother, who never walked across the lawn here, and is always here.

And somehow I remember all the dead who lie under white crosses in alien lands and their death is also in my heart, and I am at once their mother and sister and lover.

And not being a wise woman, I do not know why I am alive up here on the hill smelling the faint sweet tang of apple leaves and the soft damp odor of the ferns.

But this I know. There is something in the world of new beauty, of loveliness and of grace. There is the meaning of Stillmeadow, deep under the external, and a meaning that will go on down the deep ways of time.

There is the moment of immortality,

and this moment is tangible in the first cool crocus sturdy over a froth of snow, in the dark purple of the first glossy globe of the eggplant, and in the slow fall of the first red leaf against the breast of the autumn wind.

And after a little while, alone in the upper orchard with Honey breathing deep and soft on my hand, I know that there is actually a God, and that we, his smallest creatures, do have a meaning somehow, even if we know not why, and that love is the real and the tangible, but the rest may be a shadow in the sun, and cannot endure.

So Honey and I go down to our world again, walking through sweet fern.

And the supper lights glow from the windows of Stillmeadow.

THE END

A note on the text
Large print edition designed by
Bernadette Strickland.
Composed in 18 pt Times Roman
on a Mergenthaler Linotron 202
by Modern Graphics, Inc.